UNDERSTANDING AMERICAN FICTION AS POSTCOLONIAL LITERATURE

Literature in the Historical Development
of a Fluctuating Cultural Identity

UNDERSTANDING AMERICAN FICTION
AS POSTCOLONIAL LITERATURE
Literature in the Historical Development
of a Fluctuating Cultural Identity

Patsy J. Daniels

With a Foreword by
Shawn P. Holliday

The Edwin Mellen Press
Lewiston•Queenston•Lampeter

Library of Congress Cataloging-in-Publication Data

Daniels, Patsy J., 1944-
    Understanding American fiction as postcolonial literature : literature in the historical
development of a fluctuating cultural identity / Patsy J. Daniels ; with a foreword by
Shawn P. Holliday.
        p. cm.
    Includes bibliographical references and index.
    ISBN-13: 978-0-7734-1435-8
    ISBN-10: 0-7734-1435-5
    1. American fiction--History and criticism. 2. American fiction--Minority authors--
History and criticism. 3. Postcolonialism in literature. 4. National characteristics,
American, in literature. 5. Literature and history--United States. 6. Literature and
society--United States. I. Title.
    PS374.P635D36 2011
    813'.0093581--dc22
                                        2010049094

hors série.

A CIP catalog record for this book is available from the British Library.

Front cover: Figure of Uncle Sam courtesy of artist Dyann Gunter, 2010
Author photo: Courtesy of photographer Lois Binkley at Restored Memories Studio, TN, 2010

The Edwin Mellen Press
Box 450
Lewiston, New York
USA 14092-0450

The Edwin Mellen Press
Box 67
Queenston, Ontario
CANADA L0S 1L0

The Edwin Mellen Press, Ltd.
Lampeter, Ceredigion, Wales
UNITED KINGDOM SA48 8LT

Printed in the United States of America

For my children, who continue to inspire me.
And for my husband, Jerry Jackson, who makes it all possible.

CONTENTS

FOREWORD

In 1989, Australian scholars Bill Ashcroft, Gareth Griffiths, and Helen Tiffin published their influential book *The Empire Writes Back: Theory and Practice in Post-Colonial Literatures*, which synthesized scholarship from the 1960s, 70s, and 80s that had built the foundation for the burgeoning field of Postcolonial Studies. Their aim was to offer a comprehensive investigation of the literatures written by those who had once been colonized by Great Britain—specifically Indian, African, Caribbean, and English Commonwealth literatures—through the lens of postcolonial theory. Noticeably absent from their study was an in-depth discussion of American Literature, the term commonly used to refer to the literature of the United States. While Ashcroft, Griffiths, and Tiffin admitted that American Literature easily fit the theoretical rubric they were employing since "[…] the American experience and its attempts to produce a new kind of literature can be seen to be the model for all later post-colonial writing" (16), their brief mention of American Literature was most likely influenced by the dearth of scholarship available on the topic. Such a glaring omission was not seen as problematic since virtually no one was discussing American Literature as a postcolonial literature at that time. However, the authors missed an important opportunity to bring American Literature fully into the discussion of postcolonial theory, something that would have made their work truly groundbreaking in the late 1980s.

During the 1990s, when graduate students began reading *The Empire Writes Back* in postcolonial literature and theory courses, a few saw the absence of American Literature as a gaping flaw. This would not be easily rectified since postcolonial theory employed its own set of hegemonic practices that excluded American Literature from the accepted discourse. Many times, those who attempted to discuss American Literature within a postcolonial context were either marginalized or ignored in academe even though they were part of a growing number of disenchanted followers of postcolonial theory and its narrow political agenda. Although more than twenty years have passed since the publication of *The Empire Writes Back*, still few scholars discuss American Literature within a postcolonial context. One notable exception is Charles Baker, whose *William Faulkner's Postcolonial South* (2001) aligned Faulkner's background and intention with such "traditional" postcolonial writers as Chinua Achebe, Sean O'Casey, Ngugi wa Thiong'o, and Salman Rushdie. Another exception, the most impressive one to date, is Patsy Daniels, who has attempted to construct an all-encompassing theory of a postcolonial American Literature within this important book.

While heuristic value alone lends her book credence by offering new ways of interpreting both canonical and non-canonical texts, the scope of Daniels's study is most successful for its blending of history, culture, theory, and narrative that define American writers as having a hybrid, "split" identity with one eye focusing on the mother country and the other looking to forge a unique identity upon the North American continent. Unlike the reductive nature of most postcolonial theories, Daniels's book takes into account the complexities of America's colonial history that helps to complicate the idea of being postcolonial, thus aligning the theory with the true historical realities of most postcolonial situations. While past theorists have refused to entertain the idea of an American postcolonialism since the United States began undertaking internal imperialism of the settler nation during the late eighteenth century as well as its own brand of international imperialism during the mid-to-late-twentieth century, Daniels takes into account different phases of American history—a four-hundred-year-period marked by an ever-present flux in immigration, governmental policy, cultural acceptance, and myth-making—that has continually revised the American story. Importantly, her book helps to shed light on the processes by which third world countries become first-rate powers, thereby allowing readers to anticipate the future changes that may occur in such nations as India, Pakistan, and Iran that are slowly developing into important global players. In this way, Daniels develops Ashcroft, Griffiths, and Tiffin's notion that "[t]he first post-colonial society to develop a 'national' literature was the USA" (16). Following this early template, many postcolonial nations "[…] emerged in their present form out of the experience of colonization and asserted themselves by foregrounding the tension with the imperial power, and by emphasizing their differences from the assumptions of the imperial centre" (2). Through this process, many third-world nations now struggle to be recognized and respected on the world stage by those declining powers who were once their colonizers, the United States included.

More than anything, this book provides a new paradigm by which future scholars will begin to interpret American literature. In her discussion, Daniels widens the definition of "the colonized" to include everyone who has been culturally disenfranchised within the United States—from African Americans, Asian Americans, Native Americans, and Latinos to women, the Irish, and the Beats. She also rightly includes those early writers of the colonial period who can be counted as part of a white diaspora struggling to establish a new identity on a new continent. In this way, her book helps to realign postcolonial theory with its original aim of explaining the processes through which a colonized people attempt to regain a sense of self after colonization, extending the theory to include all colonized people, not just a chosen few. As her detailed discussion shows, the postcolonial condition is a continuous process of "becoming" through the self-awareness, realization, and motivation of a nation's artistic community.

Now that fifty years have passed since the original discussions of postcolonial theory began, it is time to extend the theory to reflect the true effects of military, economic, political, and cultural hegemony upon "other" nations and their people. This book, with its complicated look at the United States, is the first step in the right direction. With her study, Patsy Daniels shows that American Literature is, indeed, a truly postcolonial literature.

Shawn Holliday, Ph.D.
Associate Professor of English and
Associate Dean, Graduate Studies
Northwestern Oklahoma State University
Alva, Oklahoma

ACKNOWLEDGEMENTS

It is my distinct pleasure to have as colleagues and friends so many knowledgeable and astute scholars who were so willing to provide their helpful comments at various stages of the writing of this volume. My appreciation goes especially to Elizabeth Sharpe Overman, Candis P. Pizzetta, and Youngsuk Chae, friends and scholars *extraodinaire.*

The Center for University Scholars at Jackson State University provided funds for a year for a research assistant, Shuang Luo, who did an outstanding job of helping me pull my sources together. Thank you.

PREFACE, OR, WHY I WROTE THIS BOOK

Each generation has the opportunity and, indeed, the responsibility to define its own body of literature. To date, no general study of American literature of the complete twentieth century has been done. Earlier literary histories leave off at around the 1960s; after that, each literary history has focused on one theme only. This text was planned as my solution to the problem of a gap in the overview of American literary history. However, it soon became clear that what I was writing was really a theory of American fiction.

Briefly, my theory is that American fiction started as a colonial literature and has become a postcolonial literature. Initially, Americans were fearful of writing their own imaginative works in the shadow of the mother culture from England, and I propose that the same fear permeates American fiction. Many American writers have attempted to join the dominant culture through their characters; however, the definition of what American fiction is keeps changing. As well, many American writers have been excluded from the literary canon until recently, and, as the canon itself, or the definition of worthy American literature, has changed, more works from diverse points of view have been included. As the United States has grown from a group of British colonies to a major power in the world, the image that it has of itself and wants to project to the world has changed several times. In keeping up with what is "American," writers have fictionalized their own observations and experiences, to helping individuals find their identities as Americans.

Other literary histories, much larger and more detailed, are in the making, but they will be voluminous projects and will take a great deal of time to research and compose. They will doubtless include the poetry and the drama of America, genres which I almost completely ignore in this volume simply because their inclusion would prevent the timely publication of my idea. In the meantime, students of American literature can benefit from this brief history and perhaps apply the theory to poetry and drama as well. I believe that the theory could also reasonably be applied to the works of authors from other marginalized groups; one that comes to mind is what sociologists have called Appalachian whites; another is Arab American literature.

Before entering a serious discussion of American literature, it should be noted that many popular works, which are still excluded from the canon, have a great deal of influence on the American public. In this sense, the canon itself maintains the position of colonizer relative to works of popular culture. But because of their great influence on the reading public, these works may eventually find their way into the canon of so-called respectable and serious literary efforts.

However, it is the English literary canon that Americans have always held in great esteem and have attempted to emulate.

CHAPTER ONE: INTRODUCTION

. . . the search for identity is the American theme.
The nature of our society is such that we are prevented from knowing who we are.
—Ralph Ellison

Values Inherent in Literature

Everything we write is a story told from a particular viewpoint, and the author expects his or her readers to share, or at least to understand, the values presented in the fiction. And teaching literature is the teaching of values, according to Henry Louis Gates, Jr. in his 1993 *Loose Canons: Notes on the Culture Wars*, "not inherently, no, but contingently" (512); the traditional American literary canon, he writes, "represents the return of an order in which my people were the subjugated, the voiceless, the invisible, the unrepresented, and the unrepresentable" (512). Lionel Trilling had written that teaching literature is teaching culture as early as 1961. However, I contend that the cultural values presented in American fiction have been the values of the mother culture, England, and that American fiction has been, and still is, a postcolonial literature. Ashcroft, Griffiths, and Tiffin have stated that American literature can serve as the model for other postcolonial literatures (*Empire* 16).

Colonized nations are taught to revere the mother culture, and the United States has done that in many important ways. The United States has emulated England in one especially important way: it learned to colonize from its own colonizer. Not only has the United States become a colonial power, but it has also colonized what Frederic Jameson calls a "third world" within its own borders.

The United States is a country of immigrants and slaves, and American literature has a unique viewpoint because of its origin. American authors, being themselves settlers from another continent, descendants of those settlers or slaves, or later immigrants, attempt to become American, frequently through their fictional characters. As both the writers and their created characters attempt to define and become American, the country itself attempts to define itself and become America.

American Spirit versus European Spirit

In "The Dynamo and the Virgin," published in 1907, Henry Adams compares the dynamo to "a revelation of mysterious energy like that of the Cross" (99), but writes that "An American Virgin would never dare command; an American Venus would never dare exist" (100). Does this mean that Americans "knew something of the facts, but nothing of the feelings" of European culture? (99). The Virgin is mysterious and comes from the mother country; the dynamo, albeit developed through science, is likewise mysterious, and it is this kind of mystery that Americans are relegated to accept because they are cut off from the mother culture.

We might see Mark Twain's Huckleberry Finn character as a representative of the spirit of America. First, like the immigrants and slaves of America, he is an outsider. He, like America, contends with the question of slavery. But Twain's ending for the story leaves Huck's fate in a state of uncertainty. When someone else tries to force him into a mold of what he "should" be, he "lights out for the territories," a vast, amorphous space where he may be able to find his way into a new identity. In Twain's *Huckleberry Finn*, both Huck, an "uncivilized" child, and his friend Jim, a runaway slave, try to become something other than what their mother culture approves of.

In their "Introduction: Theorizing Early American Studies and Postcoloniality," Malini Johar Schueller and Edward Watts emphasize that it was a delusion that there was a stable hegemonic culture in early America. Local activities and imaginings were frequently different from those of the urban centers. The essays in *Messy Beginnings: Postcoloniality and Early American Studies*, edited by Schueller and Watts, discuss the metaphors by which the Other was denigrated and "examine aesthetic, literary, and other techniques that invoke and evoke the process of imagining which precedes and then accompanies the creation of the nation, for the marginalized, for elite whites, and for communities" (Schueller and Watts 15). In terms of regionalism, that is, regional writers when considered from the viewpoint of the Boston publishing center, "white settlers in the trans-Appalachian west felt alienated from the centralized, political, economic, and cultural centers on the east coast. By reading the action and documents of the Federalists as imperial and those of the westerners' leaders as colonial" (17), the nation can be considered "both imperial and colonial simultaneously" (18).

Their book of essays uses "postcolonial" as it describes "the struggle between imperial and local claims to cultural authority" and names "the messy processes through which an Anglophone colonial power was established and resistances to this power were articulated" (2-3). But what they consider most important is the fact that the term refers "to the analytical procedures of postcolonial studies, including that of colonial discourse analysis" (3).

Schueller and Watts explain "American Exceptionalism," and the question of whether the nation is "an extension of Europe" or whether it is "categorically separate from its purported genetic and intellectual forebears" (3). Were the states "governed by elite white males who deployed complex military and industrial technology to subdue the peoples, resources, and ideas needed to consolidate their power" while at the same time they "experimented with radical democratic ideas conceived but rarely realized in Europe," making the nation a "European colony"? (3). Or is the opposite view a more accurate depiction of the situation? It looks at "the lack of the usual markers of national identity—local language, indigeneity, shared folk traditions," suggesting that the "United States was indeed aberrant to the concept of 'nation' as it evolved in eighteenth-century Europe" (3). This view allows the European immigrants to see "their settlement as a new start—the 'city on the hill.' This idea imagines the settlements as postcolonial, models of idealized decolonization and local self-determination" (3).

But, they warn, "both 'American' and 'European' are oversimplified and under-nuanced constructions, what Gareth Griffiths has called 'fictional zones of cultural purity'" (3-4). Even though the authors "do not argue about the oppression of these groups," African Americans and "laborers, American Indians, Asian Americans, and women," they do "suggest" that these groups "persisted in questioning white male ascendancy at every moment and that their doing so was as much a part of American culture as Edith Wharton" (5). They write that "American cultural history has always been a contradictory set of narratives depicting an endless entanglement of imperial and colonial experiences and identities" (5). They agree with my thesis in stating that the essays "question the very idea of a consolidated originary vision of both a centralized national identity and a singular oppositional resistance" (6).

Comparing Schueller and Watt's ideas with Baker's concepts about the postcolonial South, they posit that "'colonized' and 'colonizing' are not mutually exclusive but rather simultaneous and contemporary" (8). They see "enormous value in recognizing the beginnings of postcolonial resistance by American Indians" (8). The "identities of the white settlers," too may have been "fundamentally shaped through encounters, appropriations, and occasionally alliances with this resistance, . . . demonstrating how natives shaped white colonial identities" as well (10).

The purpose of the book is to "give voice to the colonized populaces that voiced their resistances long before 1898 *and* to explore the local entanglements of colonial and postcolonial imperialisms, entanglements that the colonies and then the United States engaged in from the moment of white settlement" (11). They posit a "postcolonial resentment at European dismissal" of the "powerful white colonials['] . . . culture as provincial and backward" while at the same time the whites "denigrated and disciplined poor whites as well as new settlers" (12). They show that white colonization had three "economic and political" tasks: "to ensure the conquest of land from and political control over Native Americans; to secure a distinctively nonhuman form for African Americans, who could never enjoy the spoils of colonization; to legislate distinct forms of white privilege and mandate interdictions on interracial alliances so that whites could remain distinct from both American Indians and African Americans" (12-13).

The American Identity

Colonized Natives

Arriving Europeans had little concern that the continent already had several million inhabitants. They variously battled with the natives, traded with them, and treated with them. One European faction would enlist the natives to fight alongside them against another European faction. The Europeans would trade with the natives, offering concrete objects for abstract ideas, such as beads for title to the land. The natives, who still bear the label "Indians," from Christopher Columbus's mistaken idea that he had landed in India, must have thought the Europeans very gullible, since the Indians had no concept that anyone could own the land. On other occasions, Europeans would make deals with the natives that were frequently ignored when the treaties got in the way of European greed. The settlers, who considered themselves European for several generations to come, immediately set up their own culture and values as the dominant ones.

In 1682, Mary Rowlandson's "Narrative of the Captivity and Restoration of Mrs. Mary Rowlandson" was published, and, while it was an account of an actual event, it was also proof of her skill at narration and characterization. The work became one of the most popular prose works of the seventeenth century, with its adventure, heroics, and piety. It was the first and best of the "Indian captivities" that James Fenimore Cooper later transformed into works of fiction, leaving its mark on American literature as a new genre, which was, however, peculiar to North America.

In the twentieth century, Native American writer Leslie Marmon Silko shows history from the viewpoint of the victim in her story "Lullaby." In this story, the government has taken the protagonist's children away to an Indian school, and her husband and she slowly die, sitting in a snowfall. Louise Erdrich's "The Red Convertible," a story in her first novel, *Love Medicine*, is about two Native American brothers who buy a red convertible, the first convertible on the reservation. The convertible represents assimilation with the hegemony, and both brothers and car come to a sad end, with the death of the car and the corresponding suicide of one of the brothers, indicating failure at their attempted assimilation.

Colonized Africans

In 1902, W. E. B. Du Bois defines the colonized and the marginalized in *The Souls of Black Folk*, as he recalls the process by which the Negro gains meaningful liberty. "The first decade" of freedom, he writes, "was merely a prolongation of the vain search for freedom" (151); the Fifteenth Amendment subsequently gave the Negro a new ideal of liberty, and the ideal of "book-learning" became a new vision for the Negro, but prejudice against him "brings the inevitable self-questioning, self-disparagement, and lowering of ideals which ever accompany repression and breed in an atmosphere of contempt and hate" (152).

In his 1951 "Many Thousand Gone," James Baldwin states that it is when an American begins to reject all other ties and history that he becomes an American, but sarcastically points out that, after the "heathen" has been "delivered" from "shame," the American Negro must "accept that image we [Christian missionaries] then gave him of himself" (317), indicating that Americans had colonized the minds of the African slaves brought to their country. He urges equality among the races because, he writes, "Negroes are Americans and their destiny is the country's destiny" (322).

Colonized Mexicans

Sandra Cisneros, a Chicana writer, depicts the plight of the colonized Hispanics in the United States and the colonized females in her culture quite well in *The House on Mango Street*. One story in particular, "Louie, His Cousin & His Other Cousin," shows what happens to members of this culture when they attempt to join the dominant group. Louie's other cousin steals a car, a Cadillac, for a joy ride, just to see what it feels like to drive such a fine vehicle; he gives all of the neighborhood children a ride, as well. But he pays dearly for his audacity as he is arrested and hauled off to jail. They all enjoy the trappings of the hegemony, but it soon ends, and Louie's other cousin pays a heavy price.

Recovering the U. S. Hispanic Literary Heritage, edited by Ramón Gutiérrez and Genaro Padilla, is the first of many planned volumes whose "purposes include locating, rescuing from perishing, evaluating, disseminating and publishing collections of primary literary sources written by Hispanics in the geographic area that is now the United States from the Colonial Period to 1960" (13), when minority writers started to achieve some success in publication. The editors explain their use of *Hispanic*, a term which is often viewed "with a certain amount of disdain" (17), but the term, they write, "captures the history of the diaspora of Spain's peoples, institutions, and language throughout the American hemisphere," even though the label has been imposed by "outsiders" and does "tend to obliterate the diversity of Latino ethnic and national communities" (18). Hispanic literature ranges from the writings of explorers of the sixteenth century to contemporary times (Hinojosa-Smith xi).

Colonized Women

Postcolonial thought rests on feminist thought and deconstruction theory. In "Gender, Relation, and Difference in Psychoanalytic Perspective," Nancy J. Chodorow summarizes three aspects which lead to her analysis of difference and gender difference. She discusses the traditional psychoanalytic view: "when sexual difference is first seen it has self-evident value" (483). Meantime, she uses

8

Freud's "core gender identity" as another interpretation of the emergence of perceptions of gender difference. In the process of early development of core gender identity, "conflictual core gender identity problems" exist (484). While for females, difference is not originally problematic or fundamental to their psychological being or identity, "It becomes important to men to have a clear sense of gender difference, of what is masculine and what is feminine, and to maintain rigid boundaries between these" (484). Therefore, "men's and women's understanding of difference, and gender difference, must thus be understood in the relational context in which these are created" (485). Chodorow concludes that "our own sense of differentiation, of separateness from others, as well as our psychological and cultural experience and interpretation of gender or sexual difference, are created through psychological, social, and cultural processes, and through relational experiences" (486). Gender, she concludes, is learned behavior, but the effect of the patriarchy is to cause self-doubt among women and to require women to accept the image of themselves that they are given by men, much as the African slaves had been colonized.

Immigrant Literature

The place or status of the immigrant in the United States has always been amorphous, especially in the literary world. But their contributions of ethnic literature validate the concept of an American literature. Thomas J. Ferraro, in *Ethnic Passages: Literary Immigrants in Twentieth-Century America*, "contextualize[s] immigrant writers within social history" and then "examine[s] the ends to which they use variations on the up-from-the-ghetto theme" in order to "reevaluat[e] the immigrant mobility genre" (7). The presence of different ethnicities in literature allows others to become more open-minded to the life and culture of someone from a different background. The questions included in Ferraro's doubled procedure are helpful in determining the relationship of the immigrant writer to both his or her own minority culture and to the majority culture; as well, these writers must undergo a self-transformation both as immigrants and as writers.

Immigration to Cosmopolitanism

In Randolph Bourne's 1916 "Trans-National America," he states that assimilation of immigrants to the "Anglo-Saxon tradition which they unquestioningly label 'American'" (171) does not erase memories of Europe, but makes the immigrant increasingly real. After pointing out that the first foreign-born Americans were "slavishly imitative of the mother-country," he calls for "a clear and general readjustment of our attitude and our ideal" to allow the immigrant's strength to share in the direction of America in order to "save us from our own stagnation" (172). He argues that America must throw off its "nationalism of the European pattern" and become "the first international nation" (176); he urges the younger generation to accept the cosmopolitanism that has come to America and therefore to become citizens of the world (179).

In his 1941 essay "The American Century," Henry R. Luce writes that America shows signs of world leadership, but it must quit its isolationism. He urges "a vision of America as a world power which is authentically American and which can inspire us to live and work and fight with vigor and enthusiasm" (263).

Americans have always looked to England specifically and Europe generally for their culture and always try to measure up to these standards. The short story as a genre was invented largely by American authors, and this genre led to the creation of a national American literature. But the authors are self-effacing, denying their work. As American literature matured, the authors became more confident of a place in the world literature for a uniquely American literature, but their characters were still "becoming." American writers knew what it was to feel inferior, and they quite credibly wrote about that feeling by creating characters who express it.

The history of American fiction cannot be told without reference to the development of genres of fiction, the development of literary studies and literary theory, and the development of the nation itself because the nation developed at the same time the genres developed and because the development of literary studies and literary theory influenced and helped shape the United States throughout the twentieth century and continue to do so at the beginning of the twenty-first century. Charles Bernstein points out the "continuity from literary to cultural studies" (382) in the context of a collapse of the hierarchy of high and low cultures. Changes in ways of thinking not only led to new forms of literature and new ways of reading literature, but also led to new forms of government. Post-revolution America exhibited aspects of postcolonialism, and one aspect was in the perceived inferiority of its literature. Some thinkers posit that there was no American literature at all before 1800. Using colonial discourse with its postcolonial concepts as a starting point, we can see how Americans have always been "becoming."

CHAPTER TWO: THE DEVELOPMENT OF AN AMERICAN LITERATURE

. . . the secret of the American short story [is] the treatment of characteristic American life.

—Bret Harte

Beginnings

To answer the question whether there was an American literature before 1800, one must discuss a definition of both terms, *literature* and *American*. First, is literature defined by its kind of expression or by its medium of expression? If the answer is that literature is defined by its imaginative possibilities of language, then one must admit that the Native Americans had a literature before the arrival of the Europeans, even though it existed only in performance. If the answer is that literature is defined by its medium of expression, then one must agree that language preserved in letters did not exist in America before the arrival of the Europeans in the fifteenth century. But a more precise definition of American literature seems to be required; is American literature a literature *in* America, or a literature *of* America?

Even though America was populated before the arrival of Europeans, North American natives did not use a written alphabet; some historians call their expressions *orature*. In addition, the traditional European subjects of imaginative literature—love, war, chivalry, tragic grandeur, social entanglement—were deficient in the European settlements in America; consequently, opportunities as imaginative writers were reduced for the colonists. There was, therefore, little imaginative literature written in America before the nineteenth century.

However, there was a literature of America as soon as the earliest European adventurers to the "new world" were able to put pen to paper. They wrote descriptions of this continent that stirred the imaginations of individuals back home as well as the ambitions of European nations. They wrote informative briefs to sovereigns in Europe in order to influence their policymaking in regard to America. And they wrote eyewitness accounts of European devastation of the American land. Some of the early writers, such as Bernal Diaz del Castillo and John Smith, had come from the lower classes of their native countries and may never have become writers at all had not the North American continent afforded them the opportunity.

So the first writings about America were descriptions of the new world and its opportunities for European individuals and nations: letters home that described the hardships of starting life from scratch and the unfamiliarities to be found in the new environment, travel journals that described the continent itself and its natural resources to be had for the taking, and sermons and religious tracts from those settlers for whom freedom of religion was vastly important. While not all of the colonists were actively involved in religion, many of them saw the continent as a new Eden and themselves as types of Adam who had been offered a second chance.

Indeed, the early colonists were kept so busy practicing their religious beliefs and with the details of providing for their everyday needs that they could not spare time for imaginative writing, which at best was considered frivolous by most of the colonists. The earliest examples of creative writing are few and definitely far between: some poetry about daily life, a creative retelling of a kidnapping, and a sermon imaginative enough to incite a fifteen-year period of religious enthusiasm. It was not until 1650 that the first poems from America were published, those of Anne Bradstreet, and Mrs. Bradstreet's writing concerned her daily affairs: home and family and religion. In 1682, Mary

Rowlandson's "Narrative of the Captivity and Restoration of Mrs. Mary Rowlandson" was published as an account of an actual event, the most widely circulated of many such narratives. The results of Jonathan Edwards' 1741 sermon "Sinners in the Hands of an Angry God" prove not only his remarkable gift of exposition, but also of persuasion: it launched a religious fervor that lasted fifteen years and serves as a good example of English orature.

Diaries and letters abounded in early American literature. In 1650, William Bradford wrote a history of what happened to the inhabitants of Plymouth Plantation; Sarah Kemble Knight kept a diary of her hazardous round-trip journey between Boston and New York in 1704; and Quaker John Woolman kept a journal of his own travels, published in 1774, which delineates the inner life of a Quaker as well as his thoughts on the abolition of slaves. Some of the early creative writing includes a couple of fictionalized accounts of local scandals: William Hill Brown's *The Power of Sympathy* in 1789 and Hannah Webster Foster's *The Coquette or, The History of Eliza Wharton* in 1797, both written in the epistolary form that was familiar to their readership. But Foster's novel was published under a pseudonym and did not appear under her own name until almost three decades after her death.

Other writers attempted to describe or define the new nation. In 1792, an American Don Quixote story was published by Hugh Henry Brackenridge, *Modern Chivalry: Containing the Adventures of Captain John Farrago and Teague O'Regan, His servant,* showing similarities between the United States and Europe. Other early attempts to depict the new nation include Peter Markoe's 1787 *The Algerine Spy in Pennsylvania*, another epistolary novel, but this one describing America from the viewpoint of a non-Christian foreign visitor, and Royall Tyler's 1797 two-volume novel about a Boston native held captive in Algeria for six years, *The Algerine Captive*, with one volume set in the United States, the other in North Africa. Events in North Africa, or the Barbary Coast, fascinated other writers, too: Matthew Carey, whose *A Short Account of Algiers and Its Several Wars* appeared in 1794, and James Ellison, who wrote a drama,

The American Captive, or, The Siege of Tripoli, after the Tripolitan Wars were over, in 1812.

There were a couple of other creative writers who published near the end of the eighteenth century. American writer Susanna Rowson published a novel of seduction, *Charlotte Temple*, in 1791, and although it was originally published in London, it became a best-seller in the United States. In step with the Romantic movement in England, Charles Brockden Brown published no fewer than five novels in the last two years of the decade, although they were not commercial successes until they were republished, in both the United States and England, early in the nineteenth century. Benjamin's Franklin's 1818 *The Autobiography* may have been the first American book to be taken seriously by Europeans as literature, and one could speculate that his decade-long presence in Europe as the first United States Ambassador to France may have influenced the reception of his book there.

After the thirteen English colonies had become the United States of America near the end of the eighteenth century, a need arose for a national literature in order to help form a national character. Americans needed to describe themselves, but also to prove both to themselves and to Europeans that they were a "civilized" nation which was capable of producing poets, novelists, scholars, and artists who could not only express a uniquely American view, but who could also live up to world standards of literature. Although there were a few early attempts, this did not happen until after 1800.

The Novel

The development of the novel in America is traced by Cathy Davidson in *Revolution and the Word: The Rise of the Novel in America*. She shows how the development of the genre was simultaneous with changes in American society and how the novel "democratized" the minds of the American people. Because the novel was accessible to a less educated audience, and its subject might have been less than what had in the past been considered suitable, the audience was allowed or encouraged to question the authority of both the church and the state. The novel mirrored the new country in that it required "no traditional education or classical erudition" and included disparate elements. It embraced and contained "familiar literary forms such as travel, captivity, and military narratives; political and religious tracts; advice books, chapbooks, penny histories, and almanacs" (Davidson 71). Because the novel "required no knowledge of Latin or Greek, no intermediation or interpretation by cleric or academic," literate people without a classical education could have access to it. The novel was "perceived as a *subversive* literary form in every Western society into which it was introduced." It subverted concepts of "who should and should not be literate . . . what is or is not a suitable literary subject." In other words, anyone who could read had access to the novel, and the subject of the novel could be radically new. Davidson writes that the novel was an "appropriate" form for "a country first attempting to formulate itself" (71). The rise of the novel was contemporaneous with other changes in society, but it also led to the beginnings of a classless society. Even though "laws were passed in Colonial America to eliminate chapmen" who sold . . . . "street literature (crime confessions, captivity narratives, picaresque tales, etc.)" (104), these forerunners of the novel would not go away. She paraphrases Fredric Jameson's statement that "the revolution in readership signaled a larger revolution in the whole social contract of the culture" (107). As the amount of literature available for the "less educated audience" increased, the audience became "increasingly skeptical about the authority vested in minister or magistrate" (109). Thus the reader was able to serve as "an interpreter and a participant in a culture's fictions" (109). In this way the readers of the novel helped to change society.

Terry Eagleton sees a different kind of relationship between this new kind of literature and the middle class: he writes that literature was instrumental in the oppression of the middle class. Beginning with the Romantic movement, he writes, imaginative works, art, and beauty began to be seen as separate from social life (21). Both "scientific discovery and social change" caused religious ideologies to be questioned, and religion, he continues, is "an extremely effective form of ideological control" as well as "a pacifying influence" on the people (23). Literature moves in to fill the void left by religion, to "provide the social 'cement'" (23) by which a "socially turbulent class-society can be welded together" (24). As well, offering literature to the working class will keep them from demanding material goods (24-25), he writes.

Some of the earliest "literary" figures in America include Catharine Maria Sedgwick, who wrote conventional romantic novels with realistic depictions of American customs as well as feminist novels suggesting productive activities for unmarried women. Some of her romantic adventures were about colonial settlers who were either massacred or captured by American Indians (Bardes and Gossett). William Cullen Bryant, whose literary subjects were American people, living or dead, landscapes, historic events, and Indian legends, was also a lover of the classics and translated both Homer's *Iliad* and *Odyssey* (Bray).

James Fenimore Cooper was not only the first successful American novelist, but he also wrote the most important historical romance of the Revolution, the first serious American novels of manners, and the first American sociopolitical novels; he virtually created the sea novel. But Washington Irving was the first American writer with an international reputation; he wrote topical satires, biographies, and three studies of the American West. His use of realistic details contributed much to his ability to recreate history and imitate European legends in an American setting.

But it was the Romantic movement in Europe, generally dated from 1798 through 1832, that changed the definition of literature from something preserved in letters to something imaginative. In the late eighteenth and early nineteenth centuries, a revolution in European consciousness resulted in a new way of thinking, and subsequently the concept of literature shifted away from being defined by the medium of expression to being defined by the kind of expression.

During that same period, American literature was in the stage "identified by F. O. Matthiessen as the 'American Renaissance'" (qtd. in Reynolds 3); but the English Renaissance had occurred two hundred years earlier. So, by the time Americans had arrived at a written body of literature, the rules had changed, putting Americans behind again.

The Short Story

Not until the advent of that new genre, the short story, in the mid-nineteenth century did American literature begin to come into its own as a literature distinct from English literature. American authors like Hawthorne and Poe contributed greatly to the development of the short story, and, possibly because there was no European precedent for the new genre to be compared to, the European world began to acknowledge that this side of the Atlantic had something to offer in terms of literature. For example, the French held Poe in high regard both during and after his lifetime and emulated his work on the continent. Poe has long been credited with the invention of the detective story, giving the new genre of the short story a distinct subgenre that still flourishes.

But as late as 1899, American author Bret Harte wrote about the American short story from his own observations over a period of thirty years. He writes that Poe, Longfellow, and Hawthorne had lent the form "the graces of the English classics" (1357). However, he points out that the early short story in the United States was "not characteristic of American life, American habits, nor American thought . . . . Of all that was distinctly American it was evasive–when it was not apologetic" (1357). He claims that the "best writers" looked "far afield" for their subject matter or were "historical or legendary" and "seldom observant" of their own country. The American was used in a story merely "as a foil to bring into greater relief his hero of the unmistakable English pattern" (1357). He writes that no one took American literature seriously: "The old sneer 'Who reads an

American book?'," he writes, "might have been answered by another: 'There are no *American* books'" (1358).

It was only when American regional humor came to be published in newspapers that America and the American became the subject of an anecdote or story, "newspaper literature" being the "parent of the American 'short story'" (Harte 1358). But, while the Civil "war produced no characteristic American story" (1359), the California gold rush did (1360). Harte himself wrote "The Luck of Roaring Camp," a story whose "subject and character were distinctly Californian" (1361) in an attempt "to make good the deficiency" of American literature (1361). He writes that both the printer and the publisher "objected to" his story "for not being in the conventional line of subject, treatment, and morals!" (1361) because both of them were still "strongly dominated by the old conservatism and conventionalism of the East" but admits that "the critics of the Eastern States and Europe" eventually accepted it as "a new departure" (1361). Harte claims that the American short story was "the germ of American Literature to come" (1362). A study of the development of the American short story can trace the development of American literature from a colonized status to its present-day status.

American Literature as Postcolonial Literature

American literature has been colonized by Europe as well as by the university. And, as American literature has matured, it has been discovered to be something other than a monolithic unit: minority American voices have begun to be heard as they struggle against the hegemonic system which is itself still in its postcolonial mode.

American literature can be seen as a postcolonial literature when considering that its language and culture were introduced by colonists who not only had to send North American natural resources to the colonizer, but also were forced to send money in the form of taxes; the Boston Tea Party is famous as a revolt against being taxed by England. Colonization is more than economic, however; culturally, the colonizer remains the parent of the colony and retains authority in matters of values and standards. The colonized are defined by the colonizer and are made to feel different from and inferior to the colonizer.

As the colonies gradually became America, as more and more generations were born on American soil, ties to England were weakened, but not entirely severed. But this country was still considered inferior in all ways. As late as the end of the eighteenth century, Thomas Jefferson was attempting to prove to a French naturalist that the wildlife in North America were not inferior to the wildlife in Europe. He sent a large panther hide and an enormous stuffed moose to France to prove it.[1] It took so long for the United States to develop a distinctive American literature because no one in Europe took the concept seriously. Nor did the Americans themselves. American authors always looked to England for literary forms and precedents. Indeed, some of the earliest American writers, Washington Irving, Nathaniel Hawthorne, and Edgar Allan Poe, fictionalized that they had "discovered" someone else's stories, almost as if they were reluctant to publish under their own names: Washington Irving in *The Sketchbook of Geoffrey Crayon, Gent.* (1819-20), Edgar Allan Poe in "Manuscript Found in a Bottle" (1833), and Nathaniel Hawthorne in "The Custom House" (1850).

However, generating a national literature is not the same as generating respect for it. From their beginning, American universities did not teach American literature. As a matter of fact, not until the 1876 founding of Johns Hopkins University with its new "scientific" approach to higher education did

---

[1] In *Notes on Virginia,* Jefferson disputed the opinion of Georges-Louis Leclerc De Buffon, a French naturalist, that American wildlife were inferior to European; especially, he thought Buffon had "confused the red American elk with the red deer of Europe and the moose with the reindeer" (Randall 409). He sent Buffon a large "panther hide" and arranged to have an "immense moose" stuffed to send to Europe to show to Buffon (409) and to prove that American fauna were in no way inferior to European.

English as a language begin to be studied in American universities, along with other modern languages; English was not valorized above the others. When language experts later extended their study to literature by applying the science of semiotics to its analysis, it was English literature that they studied and taught, not American literature. American literature was considered inferior to English literature and was taught only in elementary and high schools and in the institutions that educated the elementary and high school teachers, women's seminaries, and institutions founded to educate the Negro. Eagleton claims that educating the middle class is not for their own benefit, but so that the middle class can control the working class (24). He writes that literature "could serve to place in cosmic perspective the petty demands of working people for decent living conditions or greater control over their own lives" (25) and keep them mollified. According to Eagleton, "It is significant, then, that 'English' as an academic subject was first institutionalized not in the Universities, but in the Mechanics' Institutes . . . . English was literally the poor man's Classics" (27).

The Morrill Act of 1862 established the land-grant universities which were to educate the "'industrial classes'" (Renker 7), and it was those students who were taught American literature. Because these inferior students were taught an inferior literature by their inferior teachers, their possibilities were extremely limited. Thus American literature served the social and political function of keeping the less-than-elite in their places and became itself a colonizing force. When American literature was finally introduced into the universities' own English departments, it was marginalized, taught in undergraduate survey courses but not in advanced undergraduate or graduate courses. Even as late as 1960, Leslie A. Fiedler chides Americans for not having a mature literature (ix). And at least one critic has stated that American literature did not become "respectable" in American universities until the 1960s (R. W. B. Lewis qtd. in Renker 2). As American literature became respectable in the universities, a literary canon was formed, consisting mostly of the works of white male writers. This canon was not questioned until the "culture wars" of the 1980s. It seems that the canon had colonized the works of women and people of color, and when works of these marginalized writers came to be read and taught by scholars, the canon was threatened.

America the Nation

But economic and political successes were important factors as well in the beginning of acceptance by the rest of the world of an American national literature. After the American Revolution separated the colonies from England and they became a new nation, and after continued "economic and political successes of the emerging nation had begun to be taken for granted, American literature as a distinct collection of texts also began to be accepted" (Ashcroft, Griffiths, and Tiffin, *Empire* 16). But the United States did not begin to distinguish itself as a world power until the Spanish-American War began in 1898, when it became itself a colonizer–of the Philippines, Guam, Puerto Rico–and the "protector" of Cuba. In 1902, Woodrow Wilson expressed his vision for the United States as a world leader, and its responsibility for the "welfare of the Philippines" played a big role in the vision; however, Wilson was still "vindicat[ing] democratic values . . . . through an overwhelmingly English frame of reference" (Hollinger and Capper 140). And Wilson explained that the reason the English settlers in North America were able to attain self-governance was their English background; he wrote, "It is thus the spirit of English life has made comrades of us all to be a nation" (Wilson 143). But the power of the United States was growing; it was American intervention in World War I that allowed the European allies to defeat Germany (Parrish xi) and, presumably, gain the gratitude of the other European countries.

New Philosophies

After Irving, Poe, and Hawthorne published their "found" stories and other stories that followed the English sensibility, the philosophies of realism and naturalism started to become apparent in short works by American authors. Realism in literature is an attempt to show real life in a realistic manner, a move away from earlier writing that placed aristocratic characters in settings that the common person would not have recognized. Realism focuses on details of dress and speech to generate a "photograph" of the scenes and characters in the minds of the readers; it was this tendency which brought about the focus on members of the lower socio-economic classes, classes which had never before been considered appropriate as subjects of imaginative writing. This shift took place in the representation of literary characters and in the literary content as the world outside the literary arena also went through significant political changes.

Malcolm Bradbury writes that in the 1890s American fiction was regarded as "an offshoot of British fiction" (v). One realistic writer, the great American novelist Henry James, whose work spanned forty years and the turn of the twentieth century, frequently depicted encounters between Americans and Europeans. But he actually lived most of his life in England and became an English citizen in 1915. According to Richard Chase, nineteenth-century American fiction "diverged from the pre-eminently social and moral direction of European fiction" (qtd. in Bradbury vi); this divergence can be seen in the realistic and naturalistic fiction written at about that time.

An early naturalistic American story is *Maggie, a Girl of the Streets*, by Stephen Crane, a story about a girl in the slums who is "ruined" and is therefore doomed to a life of prostitution. As the lower stratum of American society became subjects for imaginative writing, they began to have a voice. Stephen Crane's "The Open Boat" is a another good example of naturalism in literature. Naturalism is closely aligned with the philosophy of determinism, which holds that humans are helpless in the face of an uncaring natural environment and a frequently abusive social, economic, and political environment. Science and psychology were highly influential in this philosophy. Charles Darwin had shown the world that man is an animal, and the common man believed therefore that humans are slaves to their animal instincts. At the same time, Sigmund Freud had shown the world that man has a dark side, an unconscious, and the common man believed therefore that humans are slaves to their psyches. Put together, these two concepts demonstrated to the common man that humans have no free will. "The Open Boat" shows how men are helpless against the natural world as they escape a shipwreck on a boat; the narrator shows the agony and uncertainty that each goes through during the ordeal. Frank Norris's "A Deal in Wheat" shows how the social environment is master of the common man. In this story, Norris's protagonist goes from being a wheat farmer who is ruined by big business to an urban beggar who stands in line for free bread made from the wheat that he can no longer afford to produce. At the end of the story, the bread runs out before the protagonist gets to the head of the line; instead, he finds a notice that the bakery can no longer afford the wheat flour to make bread. At the same time, the narrator lets the reader in on the secret manipulation of the market that has ruined the farmer and turned him into a beggar. Here the working man is given a voice, and the working man may symbolize the United States as a colony. Jack London's short novel *The Call of the Wild* is another good example of naturalism in literature. The story is about a dog's life and shows how the dog moves from a comfortable existence in the home of a family to being forced to work as a sled dog in vicious conditions to finally realizing his independence and individuality as he runs away and starts his own pack. The dog is an obvious symbol of the human, and his story may indicate more than an evolution—it can also mean a move from the comfort of the parent culture to colonization to the uncertainty of independence and individual freedom, or the story of America.

Literary Studies

From realism to naturalism, from modernism to postmodernism, from stream of consciousness to the Harlem Renaissance, from agrarianism to nature writing, from feminism to ecocriticism, from multiculturalism to postcolonialism, from the beatific to magical realism, the concept of humankind's place in the world changed several times during the twentieth century. The 1970s and1980s saw a shift of critical theory from structuralism to poststructuralism, or from New Criticism to a range of other literary theories: deconstruction, new historicism, postcolonialism, feminism, ecofeminism, and culture studies among others. In the New Critical approach, which fit nicely with the tenets of modernism, the text *is* the reality, without referents, with no social or historic dimensions. However, both Marxism and feminism brought to the foreground the sociohistorical dimensions of literary texts, or what Clifford Geertz calls "thick description." Poststructuralism agrees that the text is the reality, but the text has been extended to mean the whole world. Now it is seen that literary work must be practiced in and through various institutional forms that Jerome J. McGann calls "mediational structures" (4-5) outside the work itself, such as the publishers, the academy, the church, and the courts. One thread seems to run through the literature of the twentieth century, however—the search for an identity. This quest becomes a motif in the stories and novels of major writers: the identity of the individual, the identity of the community, and, indeed, the identity of the nation. As the characters in the fiction of twentieth-century America attempt to become "American," the concept of what "American" is keeps changing.

In the 1920s there emerged a new generation of American writers, the modernists, "whose work seemed to have world impact[,] . . . creating both a usable present and a sense of a usable past" (Bradbury v). In 1930 Sinclair Lewis received the Nobel Prize for Literature, the first American to do so, indicating a change in the world's view of American literature. As modernism entered the literary mainstream, Sherwood Anderson showed his *Winesburg, Ohio* characters to be repressed by society, but when these characters attempt to decolonize themselves, to exhibit some individuality, they all come to some bad end. One of the first stories about a woman of color is "Melanctha" in *Three Lives* by Gertrude Stein, an American writer, indeed, but an American writer who lived in Europe for most of her life. So, even as she gives a voice to Melanctha, she is immersed in European sensibilities.

According to Martin Halliwell in *American Culture in the 1950s*, "modernism implies a continual reassessment of the past in light of the ever-changing present" (242). Modernism as a literary movement encompassed experimentation with literary forms; coming as it did on the heels of realism and naturalism, one experimental form of expression which might have been expected was stream-of-consciousness writing, or the representation of the thoughts of the characters, going deeper into the character than merely describing clothing, activities, or speech. Modernism, while it included many kinds of formal literary innovation, also encompassed a reaction to science and technology. Postwar modernism, as seen in such works as Kurt Vonnegut, Jr.'s *Slaughterhouse-Five*, reflected the prevailing sense of fragmentation and disillusion. Other characteristics of later modernism are increasing self-awareness, introspection, and openness to the unconscious and to humanity's darker fears and instincts.

So-called "high" modernism was a literary expression for the elite, the educated. It was so "high" that its proponents would include many references to classical works, frequently untranslated from Greek or Latin; it was during this movement that literary criticism came into its own, as it was necessary to analyze and explain what each work meant. The rise of the literary magazine occurred during the same period; the magazines were so successful because they printed not only literary works, but also an explanation of them.

Literary criticism became formalized at this time; indeed, a group of students and professors at Vanderbilt University published a formal method of analyzing literature. It is called New Criticism because it was new at the time, during the 1930s, and is based on the idea that a work of literature can be valued in and of itself, just as any other work of art can, a painting, or a vase, for example. One of them, Cleanth Brooks, published the *Well-Wrought Urn*, in which he advocated looking only at the text, comparing a literary text to an urn. Most educated people are familiar with this kind of literary criticism because it was the only one used for about forty years in the United States, and most of them were exposed to it in high school. Readers would recognize the search in the text for symbols and images, the discernment of the plot and setting, characterization and irony, and so on. This kind of literary analysis went hand-in-hand with high modernism; it showed readers who did not have an education in the classics how to figure out what the high modernists were saying.

Some of those less-educated people were immigrants. New immigrants from Eastern and Southern Europe were stranded in what David Roediger calls an "inbetween" social stratum, but they emerged to assimilate into the dominant culture. He calls attention to matters of identity: individual, community, and national. Along the way, he castigates Theodore Roosevelt and the "New Deal liberals" as being, while perhaps not initiators, certainly perpetrators of the situation. Immigration laws changed in 1898 to stop counting immigrants by nationality, as had been done in the past, and to begin counting them according to "race." Italians, Greeks, Poles, and Hungarians were required to prove their "whiteness," which seems to mean their worthiness to become part of the hegemony. The new immigrants became racially conscious in the United States as they had never needed to be in Europe. While they coexisted with African Americans, they soon learned that they must prove themselves "better" than Americans of African ancestry by imitating the dominant culture's discrimination against that group. National leaders opined openly that the new immigrants may be considered white after two or three generations of social and educational change and perhaps some intermarrying. It seems that "white" had become the definition of "American."

Technology and consumerism brought about their own changes. The suburban house had become a critical symbol of consumer prosperity and fulfillment both in popular literature and in advertising by the 1920s. The building of single-family homes slowed significantly during the Great Depression and war, but boomed again in the postwar fifties. The suburban ideal was an ideal not only of neighborhood, but also of domestic life. Therefore, the residents sought not only an individual identity through self-reflection in this place of social and economic change, but also a social identity as they communed with like-minded neighbors who were in the same social class. Twentieth-century American novels critique the borderland culture of the suburbs; rather than agreeing that the suburban lifestyle represents the American Dream, novelists represent suburbia as a place of "mass production, standardization, dullness, and conformity" (Jurca 6); therefore, the residents in these novels feel victimized. Typical suburbanites were trapped in their own homes and in neighborhoods of their own making. Suburban homes are really just houses, not homes, and suburbanites may be homeowners, but they are in reality homeless, according to Jurca. Modern advertising and consumer culture caused the suburbanite to experience a lack of emotional or spiritual fulfillment rather than finding comfort in ownership and in ownership as a mark of identity. The city in these novels is a colonizing force that the suburbs must be on the alert for.

As the world changed, however, ways of expression changed as well. Writers respond to their environment, and it becomes necessary to find new ways to express new ideas. A major change in the United States, which, by the way, was reflected in colonies the world over, came in the 1960s with the civil rights movement and the civil rights laws which were enacted in the mid-1960s. As African American citizens gained or re-gained the right to have a voice in the government, European colonies on the African and South American continents were gaining independence from their colonizers. Of course, these events either precipitated or were the result of a major shift in thinking, in perceiving the world and humans' place in it. Those who brought about the change were the creative thinkers, those who could imagine a different way of living, of relating to the world. As many of them committed these ideas to print, literary expression reflected the change. The idea of a postmodernism emerged, which challenged the philosophy and practices of modern arts or literature. Some critics believe that postmodernism is an extension of modernism; others see it as an entirely different way of conceiving the world. It can be said, however, that the postmodernist movement in literature is at least partially characterized by the notion of alienation; alienation from the dominant culture is what many of the thinkers and writers during mid-century were expressing. They reacted against an ordered view of the world as well as against traditional literary forms. This reaction can be seen in different styles of writing that use parody and in the rise of "such concepts as the absurd, the antihero and the antinovel, and magic realism" ("Postmodern" 899). Because meaning was perceived to be relative, new ways of understanding texts arose as poststructuralism and new critical theories abounded, especially those based on deconstruction.

The Marxist system of thought explained economic classes and the struggles of the lower classes; biologists had been unable to locate a species, or racial, difference in humans. Groups which had been marginalized by the dominant culture began to clamor for a voice. Women once again sought to be treated as citizens equal to men; other minority groups in the United States renewed their claim as part of the citizenry. They found allies in members of the dominant culture, especially in the counterculture movement of the 1960s and 1970s. The literature produced by these writers demonstrated the strength and fortitude of those descendants of immigrants, and also showed familial relations within these cultures. The introduction of these minority authors showed an evolution in the acceptance into the literary world. Thinkers from abroad like Michel Foucault and Jacques Derrida influenced American thinkers. As a new vision of the world emerged, so did a new way of writing, a new subject matter of literature, and a new way of analyzing literature.

In contemporary literary criticism, there are many approaches, but each one is not necessarily applicable to every work of literature, as had been the case with New Criticism. Briefly, they include Marxism, feminism, new historicism, postcolonialism, multiculturalism, deconstruction, to name only a few. Now literature could be approached by looking at power structures and the working conditions of the characters, by looking at the treatment of female characters, by looking at the social milieu surrounding both the setting of the literature and its publication, by looking at characteristics of the writings of formerly colonized peoples, by looking at the literatures of other cultures, and by turning it all inside out through deconstruction. Literary criticism has never held that there is a single valid interpretation of any work; one valid interpretation does not preclude another valid interpretation. Because authors strive for ambiguity, or the depth of meaning arrived at by making one thing stand for two meanings, literature has many levels of meaning and therefore of interpretation.

The Twentieth Century and Beyond

Just as Ashcroft, Griffiths, and Tiffin have defined characteristics of postcolonial literature, so W. E. B. Du Bois defined the characteristics of colonization in a more personal manner. In *The Souls of Black Folk* he wrote that the prejudice against "the Negro" causes "the inevitable self-questioning, self-disparagement, and lowering of ideals" which appear in colonized cultures (152); in other words, prejudice produces a personal feeling of inferiority in the colonized. William Faulkner was a modernist writer who chose as one of his themes the fall of the Southern aristocracy with the concomitant pain of the postbellum period. The South was colonized by the North when the Union overcame Southern resistance during the Civil War. During the period of Reconstruction, the former Confederate States were further colonized by the United States troops sent to occupy the South. Faulkner offers an apology of sorts in his story "A Rose for Emily," as the narrator shows the madness of the title character and implicates the townspeople in the action of the story, as they had supported the notion of her aristocracy. In his "Barn Burning," Faulkner shows the plight of the white sharecropper in competing with former slaves for work, even though Abner Snopes, the antagonist of this piece, is not a sympathetic character. Katherine Anne Porter's "The Fig Tree" views the South's attempts at growing up through the eyes of the young protagonist, Miranda, even as hints of lynching lurk in the background of the story. As well, another Southern writer, Eudora Welty, shows the plight of the poor black woman in "A Worn Path," an allusion to the myth of Sisyphus, who gets nowhere from his struggles. Richard Wright, in "Almos' a Man," demonstrates the desperation of a young black man who is attempting to grow up; he stands for all of the African Americans of the time as well as for the whole nation, which is still attempting to locate its maturity.

Although a few Native American novels had been published earlier in the twentieth century, it was not until after the civil rights movement and the student activism of the 1960s and the second feminist movement, in the 1970s, that imaginative works by writers from minority cultures in the United States began to be published and read. Publishing novels from previously silenced writers led to what has been called the "culture wars," in which one scholar famously warned that universities were substituting Alice Walker for Shakespeare, Alice Walker being the writer thrice-colonized by being American, black, and female, and Shakespeare the white male writer from England, the mother culture.

However, Americans are still insecure regarding their artistic standing in the world. For example, The National Endowment for the Humanities' 37th Jefferson Lecture in the Humanities delivered by John Updike on May 22, 2008 is entitled "What is American about American Art?" and was summarized by Jennifer Howard for *The Chronicle of Higher Education*. She writes, "Much of the story Mr. Updike told was a familiar one, of a young country drawing its inspiration from nature and from commerce and always looking over its shoulder at Europe" and continues that it was not until the "mid-20th century" that the United States gained "artistic independence." It seems that the ghost of Europe still haunts Americans, many of whom still carry that feeling of not being good enough.

But some people still view anything British, even low-class British, as superior to anything American. A case in point is the recurring use by many educated Americans of the particle *an* in front of *historical*. English grammar calls for the use of *a* in front of a consonant sound as in *historical* and the use of *an* in front of a vowel sound, the sound one would achieve by dropping the *h* in *historical*. Dropping the initial *h* is characteristic of the lowest-class dialect of England, yet some Americans prefer to imitate this dialect because it sounds British and therefore indicates superiority.

As far as the status of American literature in the university, an article in the *New York Review of Books,* "The Decline and Fall of Literature" by Andrew Delbanco, says it all: ". . . everybody knows that if you want to locate the laughingstock on your local campus these days, your best bet is to stop by the English department." Even though American literature has become accepted in the university, the department which houses it remains marginalized. As well, Delbanco points out that "the laughter . . . is not confined to campuses" and gives the example of *The New York Times'* "holiday ritual" of printing "a derisory article" in "deadpan *Times* style" about the annual Modern Language Association's convention which for decades met over the Christmas holidays, at which scholars of literature and languages from the world over come to share their thoughts with their colleagues. But, if the *New York Review of Books* and *The New York Times* both are making fun of the discipline and its professors, the question remains whether American literature is taken seriously by anyone in the United States besides those whose employment depends upon it.

And the status of American literature in the world is still unstable. In a 2008 Associated Press story, the permanent secretary of the Swedish Academy, Horace Engdahl, made the comment, regarding selection of that year's Nobel

Prize for Literature, that Americans are "handicapped" in terms of winning the prize. He explains:

> Of course there is powerful literature in all big cultures, but you can't get away from the fact that Europe still is the center of the literary world . . . not the United States . . . . The U. S. is too isolated, too insular. They don't translate enough and don't really participate in the big dialogue of literature. That ignorance is restraining.

But his remarks were disputed by two important Americans in the same article, which appeared in *The Washington Post*. David Remnick, editor of the *New Yorker,* defended American literature in his response to Engdahl's remarks: "And if he looked harder at the American scene that he dwells on, he would see the vitality in the generation of Roth, Updike and DeLillo, as well as in many younger writers, some of them sons and daughters of immigrants writing in their adopted English." And Harold Augenbraum, executive director of the National Book Foundation, explained that American literature has become great through immigration. "Each generation," he notes, "beginning in the late 19th century, has re-created the idea of American literature." But it seems that Americans still cannot convince the rest of the world that American literature is world class.

CHAPTER THREE: THEORY

As soon as you ask the question "Who am I?" you are an American.
—Gish Jen

Social Agendas

Jane Tompkins sees literary texts as "attempts to redefine the social order" (xi) and indicates that it is the purpose of the novel to change culture. Noam Chomsky has written about the role and responsibility of intellectuals; during the Vietnam War era, he wrote that it is the responsibility of intellectuals "to speak the truth and expose lies" (456). John M. Ellis argues that affirmative action has turned literary criticism into social activism and that the traditional defense of the humanities, that "the humanities enabled us to see ourselves in perspective, to become more enlightened citizens, and to think more deeply about important issues in our lives" (3), has been abandoned in favor of social activism. He claims that current literary theories are really social agendas. Scholars that he calls "race-gender-class scholars" question the existence of objective knowledge. He writes that they "argue that objectivity and truth are naive illusions of traditional scholars" and that "all knowledge is socially constructed" (191). George Levine also shows a relationship between the social and the literary; he writes, "Psychology, through Freud and Lacan in particular, infects the thinking of social scientists and humanists; philosophy becomes literary theory which becomes cultural study" (2). Part of cultural study is the idea of postcolonialism, and part of the postcolonial condition is an "intense hostility to the self" (7). Levine indicts the language of the colonizer that the colonized must use; he writes that the "shaping forces" of this self-hatred "are not outside us, they are inside us, in the systems, particularly of language, that shape our imaginations and our thought" (7).

Definition of Terms

The best attempt to define postcolonialism is found in the 1989 *The Empire Writes Back*, a seminal work by Bill Ashcroft, Gareth Griffiths, and Helen Tiffin. In it, these authors name "three important features of all post-colonial writing," which are "The silencing and marginalizing of the post-colonial voice by the imperial centre; the abrogation of this imperial centre within the text; and the active appropriation of the language and culture of that text" (83).

Critics make a distinction between the practice of imperialism and the later practice of colonialism. Ashcroft, Griffiths, and Tiffin, internationally recognized exponents of postcolonial theory, write that one must define *colonialism* by first defining *imperialism*, and then they quote Edward Said regarding the way colonialism is a part of imperialism. *Imperialism*, according to Said, refers to "a dominating metropolitan centre ruling a distant territory," but *colonialism*, "which is almost always a consequence of imperialism, is the implanting of settlements on distant territory" (qtd. in *Key Concepts* 40). And, they point out, whereas imperialism is ancient, colonialism came later and is a "specific form of cultural exploitation that developed with the expansion of Europe over the last 400 years" (40). *Postcolonialism* "deals with the effects of colonization on cultures and societies," they write (168). While "colonial discourse theory" was developed in the writings of critics like Said, Gayatri Spivak, and Homi Bhaba, the term *postcolonial* was first used by Spivak in her 1990 publication *The Post-Colonial Critic* (168).

As well, scholars have debated whether the hyphen should be used in the spelling of the word. In their 2007 *Post-Colonial Studies: The Key Concepts*, Ashcroft, Griffiths, and Tiffin explain that originally the hyphen was used in order to "distinguish post-colonial studies as a *field* from colonial discourse theory *per se*, which formed only one aspect of the many approaches and interests that the term 'post-colonial' sought to embrace and discuss" (168-69). They continue:

> "Post-colonialism" is now used in wide and diverse ways to include the study and analysis of European territorial conquests, the various institutions of European colonialisms, the discursive operations of empire, the subtleties of subject construction in colonial discourse and the resistance of those subjects, and, most importantly perhaps, the differing response to such incursions and their contemporary colonial legacies in both pre- and post-independence nations and communities. While its use has tended to focus on the cultural production of such communities, it is becoming widely used in historical, political, sociological and economic analyses, as these disciplines continue to engage with the impact of European imperialism upon world societies. (169)

As well, now we speak of both neo-colonialism and cultural imperialism. *Neo-colonialism*, according to Lois Tyson, is the idea that international corporations practice a similar kind of subjugation of vulnerable nations in terms of politics, economics, and culture (425). *Cultural imperialism* is the effect that one culture, specifically American, has upon another culture, perhaps India, which consumes the artifacts of American culture; for example, American dress, music, and movies (425-26).

The History of Postcolonial Thought

Edward Said and Gayatri Spivak are generally acknowledged as the leaders in postcolonial thought. In his 1978 *Orientalism*, Said explained how the colonizer invents the colonized, attributing to the colonized characteristics that are opposite to the characteristics of the colonizer, thus defining both the colonizer and the colonized; he used as an example his own experiences as a Palestinian who had to flee from his homeland as the Israelis took over. Spivak came to postcolonialism through feminism; as she saw women treated as second-class citizens, she extended that line of thought to include her own country of India as the second-class citizens relevant to the English colonizers of India. In her 1983 lecture, "Can the Subaltern Speak?" she concluded that the subaltern, or the oppressed, has no voice in public affairs.[2]

However, they were not the first to voice these observations. Chinua Achebe, a Nigerian educated in an English institution, challenges colonial myths in his first novel, *Things Fall Apart*, published in 1959. In it, he gives his Igbo characters an individuality that Joseph Conrad, representing the colonizer, had not in his 1899 novel about European colonization of Africa, *Heart of Darkness*. Achebe does so again in his important 1977 essay, "Image of Africa: Racism in Conrad's *Heart of Darkness*." Frantz Fanon's *The Wretched of the Earth*, published in 1961 and translated into English in 1963, was an early treatise against colonialism that also argued the importance of nationalism in throwing off the colonizer. He was born in a French colony, the French Antilles, and was influenced by the *négritude* movement from the 1940s and 1950s. *Négritude* was a movement promoting a black identity, and its leaders, Aimé Césaire, Léon Damas, and Léopold Sédar Senghor, were from French colonies: Martinique, French Guyana, and Senegal, respectively. They were inspired by the Harlem Renaissance and influenced by French existentialism.

Ngugi wǎ Thiong'o, Taban lo Liyong, and Henry Owuor-Anyumba iterate the political uses of education and openly call for the abolition of the English Department in their famous 1968 postcolonial essay, "On the Abolition of the English Department." In this essay, the authors, from Kenya, Uganda, and Kenya, respectively, show how their cultures have been colonized not only by the English language, but also by English literature itself, as universities hold English

---

[2] The lecture was subsequently revised and expanded in 1999 as part of her *Critique of Postcolonial Reason*.

literature up as the literature to be revered and emulated because it is from the mother culture, England.

And other theorists have extended the ideas of Said, Spivak, and their forerunners. In her 1987 article "Post-Colonial Literatures and Counter-Discourse," Helen Tiffin defines "the project of post-colonial writing" as "to interrogate European discourses" and "to investigate the means by which Europe imposed and maintained" its own values on "so much of the rest of the world" (95). These are subversive maneuvers and are "characteristic of post-colonial texts" (95), she writes. She proposes two "models for future post-colonial studies" (96): one which investigates the content and the other which investigates the means of production of colonial literature.

Homi K. Bhabha expands on the work of Said and Spivak by using Jacques Derrida's theory of deconstruction, specifically the concept of binary oppositions, to propose that cultures are hybrid rather than fixed. He argues that cultures are manufactured rather than spontaneously appearing out of some innate qualities. His most important work is his 1989 essay, "The Commitment to Theory," which defines hybridity as not the one and not the other.

In *U. S. Orientalisms: Race, Nation, and Gender in Literature, 1790-1800,* Malini Johar Schueller writes that she departs "from Said's theoretical formulations . . . in pursuing issues of gender from a feminist and non-heterosexual imperative" (5); as well, she does not see "Oriental discourses within the United States" as "unchanging," as Said does in his original statements of his postcolonial theories (5) regarding "largely. . . the Muslim Near and Middle East" (6). She agrees, however, that Said has made it "impossible to think about Western constructions of the Orient in purely spiritual, philosophical, or symbolic terms . . . [and has made it] problematic to deal with any construction of an Other without thinking about relations of power" (6).

Schueller's 1998 book title, *U. S. Orientalisms,* after both Said and Michel Foucault, indicates her "need to open up these terms to the possibility both of different kinds of literary Orientalisms and of different kinds of discourse on the

Orient" (7). She begins with a poem from the American Revolutionary period, written by Timothy Dwight and published in 1780, "America, or a Poem on the Settlement of the British Colonies, Addressed to the Friends of Freedom and Their Country" (1) and shows how the poem predicts the future of the new country as glorious, "tracing the beginnings of civilization in Asia." The poet "prophesies the glory of the nation as it imperialistically extends its dominion" through "the goddess of freedom," in a "dream vision" (1).

Schueller moves on to a discussion of American literature of the last few years of the eighteenth century, much of which focused on the United States' relations with the Muslim states of North Africa which resulted in the Tripolitan Wars of 1801-1805: Royall Tyler, James Ellison, Washington Irving, Matthew Carey, and Peter Markoe. She shows how the image of the United States is set forth as a place of refuge, "a haven for the persecuted," and is shown to have "a command over the Orient" (1). She limits her discussion to the century between 1790 and 1890, but provides a solid base for a discourse on the United States as the hegemonic culture against the cultures of the Other that we attempt to update in our own work.

In *The Empire Writes Back: Theory and Practice in Post-colonial Literatures*, Bill Ashcroft, Gareth Griffiths, and Helen Tiffin suggest that "the American experience and its attempts to produce a new kind of literature can be seen to be the model for all later post-colonial writing" (16) and give India as an example of including "indigenous Indian english [sic] texts" in their schools (217-18, n. 1). As well, they iterate three important features of all postcolonial writing (83), showing that former colonies in Africa, Asia, and the Americas all "write back" to the empire in similar ways even though their experiences of colonization have been individually separate and distinct.

In Brazilian Paulo Freire's 1993 *Pedagogy of the Oppressed*, he sees a decolonizing solution for the oppressed. Freire points out that the educational practices of the oppressor extend and propagate oppression by what he calls the "banking" approach to teaching, in which the teacher fills the empty student with knowledge. In a colonial world, the student is the colony and the teacher the mother culture. Freire recommends a teaching methodology that liberates the illiterate by posing problems and drawing the student into a dialogue with the teacher. He points out that the oppressors are themselves negatively influenced by their own oppressive actions and suggests that "It is only the oppressed who, by freeing themselves, can free their oppressors. The latter, as an oppressive class, can free neither others nor themselves. It is therefore essential that the oppressed wage the struggle to resolve the contradiction in which they are caught; and the contradiction will be resolved by the appearance of the new man: neither oppressor nor oppressed" (38). [3]

In Terry Eagleton's *Literary Theory: An Introduction* he writes that the "universal human values" found in literature can keep "civil wars, the oppression of women or the dispossession of the English peasantry" at the level of "historical trivia" (25), and that literature could quiet the demands of the working people for greater control of their own lives by giving them a greater perspective that make their own miseries seem petty (25). Thus the political power of literature.

---

[3] As an aside, it is interesting to note that while these postcolonial thinkers speak from their own experiences as part of a colonized culture, every one of them has been educated, at least in part, in the language of and the institutions of the colonizer. Chinua Achebe was educated at University College in Ibadan, where he received an undergraduate degree, but, at the time, University College was associated with the University of London. Frantz Fanon, from the French Antilles, was trained as a psychiatrist in Lyon, France. Ngugi was educated at Makerere University in Uganda and at Leeds University in England. Taban lo Liyong earned the B.A. from the Ugandan National Teachers College and then graduated from the writer's workshop at the University of Iowa. Owuor-Anyumba earned a teaching degree from the University of East Africa and a B.A. from Cambridge University in England.

Edward Said was a Palestinian whose family fled to Egypt when the Israelis captured his homeland, West Jerusalem, and ultimately moved to the United States for an education at Princeton and Harvard. Gayatri Chakravorty Spivak, from India, took the B.A. from the University of Calcutta and then the M.A. and Ph.D. in English literature from Cornell University. Homi K. Bhabha earned the B.A. from Bombay University and then the M.A., M.Phil., and D.Phil. from Oxford University in England. Paulo Freire was educated at Recife University, Brazil, a former Portuguese colony, and Ashcroft, Griffiths, and Tiffin are all from Australia, a former British colony.

But now there is another way to control the masses. In 1962, German theorist Jürgen Habermas published *The Structural Transformation of the Public Sphere: An Inquiry into a Category of Bourgeois Society*, which was translated into English in 1989. In it, Habermas claims that the public sphere, which once consisted of discussions and debates about public matters, both face to face and in writing, and was a vital counterbalance to political authority, is now an illusion. No longer does the public participate in real discussions relevant to democracy, politics, or governmental authority; instead, the public is the passive recipient of reports on celebrity activities, advice, catchy labels, and "infotainment," which encourages journalists toward sensationalism as they compete against each other in the entertainment marketplace. In this way, the whole of the bourgeoisie is held down and prevented from taking part in public affairs, even in the land of the colonizer. Habermas sees a responsibility for the intellectuals in such a milieu to promote "communicative action."

CHAPTER FOUR: UNITED STATES HISTORY IN BROAD STROKES

[O]ur modern writers have had to discover and recover and chart the country in every
generation . . . [and] must still cry America! America!
As if we had never known America.
                                                                        –Alfred Kazin

Colonization, or Becoming America

When Europeans discovered the Americas, they saw great possibilities for themselves. This "new" world had many natural resources which had never been used as the Europeans would have used them. Not the least of these resources were the virgin forests with their tall trees, perfect for building the wooden ships that European navies and long-distance commerce depended upon. Since wooden ships sink or burn at rates faster than trees can be grown, the Europeans saw the Americas as a source of materials with which to renew their sea-going assets. The spaciousness of the continents, too, invigorated the European imagination. Since their populations kept growing but their geographic locations remained the same size, Europe was becoming a tight fit. Not only was European space limited, but the land was held in but a few hands. The landowners were the ones whose culture was dominant. Those multitudes who owned no land had little hope that they ever could own land and would therefore forever remain subservient to the dominant culture. However, the Americas could alleviate that situation: in the "new" world, every man could have his own land and gain freedom from oppression. This may have been the beginning of the "American Dream."

There was great competition among European nations regarding who would control which part of the continent. The Dutch made inroads in what is now New York, but were eventually ousted by the English. As well, the French colonized much of what is now Canada, but their control was limited by the English to the area which is now Quebec. The Spanish took over what we call Central America and the current United States Southwest, as well as parts of the Gulf Coast, notably present-day Florida and Louisiana. The French eventually came to control Louisiana, and even sold it (along with lots of other territory) to the new United States in the form of the Louisiana Purchase.

Not to be ignored is the slave trade which flourished for several hundred years between Africa and the "new" world. Africans were brought to the Americas against their will and under conditions so harsh that many of them perished during the voyage. Their lives as slaves meant that they had no freedom to make decisions, to care for their families, or even to establish families. There was now a new aspect to being American.

The literature of the early period was not imaginative literature, but mainly consisted of reports back to Europe about what the explorers had found and descriptions of the land. However, many reports exaggerated the riches to be had, which enticed other Europeans to leave their homes for a new life on the new-found continent. Some of the Europeans came to the new continent so that they could get away from the religious persecution that they suffered in their home countries. Therefore, much of the early literature appeared in the form of sermons and religious tracts. The settlers had to spend so much time and energy on taking care of their daily needs, finding materials for building shelters, finding or growing food, making fabric with which to make their clothing, making soap with which to wash their clothes, and either "Christianizing" or fighting the Indians, that they had little time for writing.

The idea of America, then, took shape from colonization by European nations which squabbled amongst themselves over the riches and land to be had on the continent and came to include both African slaves and American Indians, who had been colonized from the day the Europeans set foot on the continent.

Revolution, or Becoming American

Eventually, though, the lives of the settlers stabilized to the extent that they could think of things other than daily existence, and, at the same time, new generations were born, generations who had never seen Europe and had little allegiance to that faraway land. From 1620, when the Mayflower landed, until 1776, the beginning of the Revolutionary War, we can count 156 years; allowing for 20 years per generation, we can count almost eight generations born on the new continent. That would be the great-great-great-great-great-grandchildren of the original voyagers. By then, the old country had likely become a myth as far as allegiance, even though English ways and values still persisted. For example, there was still a distinction between the elite ruling class and the common people. Even though there was no monarch, certain educated, land-holding individuals held the power. These elite became known as the Founding Fathers, and they are the ones who wrote not only the Declaration of Independence but also the other founding documents of the new nation. They are the ones whose culture other Americans were expected to emulate. It was not until 1829, another 53 years, or almost three more generations, that a representative of the common man, Andrew Jackson, was elected as leader. In less than two more generations, or during the lives of Jackson's grandchildren, the states underwent a great rift, which today we call the Civil War. The idea of what America should be was the basis of the war, and both sides called themselves Americans, even though their worldviews and values differed enough to kill and be killed for.

The Postbellum Period

As could be expected, there was much writing during the period leading up to the war which espoused the views of one side or the other; each side was passionate in presenting its arguments for what the country should be. One piece of imaginative writing stands out in this period, however, Harriet Beecher Stowe's *Uncle Tom's Cabin.* In this novel, Stowe describes characters that represent the many different ways of looking at the disagreements; it could almost be called an allegory. The book was not as successful as a novel as it was as a piece of propaganda, though. Stowe appealed to the mothers regarding the abolition of slavery, even though those mothers, being colonized by means of their gender, could not make decisions by way of the vote. They could, however, bring pressure to bear on their fathers, brothers, husbands, and sons to favor abolition, so much so that President Abraham Lincoln famously called Stowe "the little woman who started the big war."

Not much imaginative literature was written during the five years of the Civil War; everyone was too involved in the war, especially in the South, on whose land the war was fought, to record imaginative thoughts. But, according to Charles Baker, no Southerner wrote anything at all about the period of Reconstruction, from 1865 through 1877, when Union soldiers occupied the South. However, when Southerners began to write imaginative literature again, it was as postcolonial writers. In his discussion of William Faulkner and postcolonialism, Baker writes that the South was colonized by the North and that subsequent literature to come out of the South exhibits postcolonial characteristics. At the same time, he notes, Faulkner himself was of the group, white Southern males, who colonized those beneath them, women and African Americans, while at the same time suffering the oppression of the defeated. This situation adds the colonized South to the increasingly diverse nature of the American identity.

American Imperialism

Barely three decades after the Civil War, the United States found itself embroiled in another war, but this was one in which soldiers who had recently fought against each other faced a common rival. In this war, the Spanish-

American War, the United States effectively removed Spain as a colonizer of Cuba, Puerto Rico, Guam, and the Philippines. However, instead of granting freedom to these people as the United States had purported to do, the United States installed itself as the colonizer of the same areas. Even though the United States was ostensibly fighting for the freedom of the Spanish colonies, it became a *de facto* colonizer. In becoming a colonizer, the United States, former English colony, paid the ultimate compliment to the English culture that it so greatly admired in a way that also made the United States an international force.

The Turn of the Twentieth Century

At the beginning of the twentieth century, American fiction was energized by the concepts of realism, naturalism, and determinism. Realism as a literary movement started in the late nineteenth century and was based on a simplification of style and image and an interest in poverty and everyday concerns. Authors attempted to describe in minute detail the settings and the characters in their fiction, even the way the characters spoke. Especially of interest was the way the uneducated spoke and the poor lived. Naturalism was also a late nineteenth-century movement; proponents of this movement believed heredity and environment, both areas studied as sciences, control people. Determinism, or the idea that everything has already been determined, is closely associated with naturalism, as it was believed that heredity could not be changed. Together they presented the concept that the disadvantaged were different from those for whom the authors wrote and that the poor and uneducated could not change their circumstances. Literary analysis at the time consisted mainly of comparing each work with other works by the same author, or perhaps with contemporary literary works by another author.

The theories of both Darwin and Freud were influential, and there was a popular belief that science and scientific method could solve social problems.

Henry Adams famously compared technological advancement with a spiritual force behind the culture in his "The Dynamo and the Virgin" (97). This era gave rise to social work as an area of endeavor as well as to other measures of social reform, including Prohibition and women's right to vote. However, a literacy test effectively kept blacks from voting. According to historian John Milton Cooper, Jr., "black Americans suffered segregation, discrimination, disenfranchisement, racist political demagoguery, and racial violence that nearly always went unpunished and often won applause from whites" (xiii), demonstrating their thorough oppression even though blacks had won the right to vote.

The Progressive era, a period of reform from the 1880s to the 1920s in which thrived "grand progressive designs to make over America or the world," is described by Michael E. Parrish in his discussion of the two decades comprising the years 1920 through 1941 (8). Parrish writes, "In these years, American had to cope both with unprecedented economic prosperity and the worst depression in their history" (x). These two decades "saw the maturation and temporary collapse of a full-blown, consumer-oriented economy that profoundly affected the physical welfare and moral sensibilities" of every United States citizen. As well, the "deprivations of the 1930s left no facet of American society–productive relations, race relations, or gender relations–untouched" (x). He explains, "Traditional American cultures, anchored to particular ethnic communities, religious traditions, and geographic places, faced absorption or dilution in a sea of standardized products and homogenized attitudes spread by manufacturers, advertisers, the airwaves, and the silver screen" (x). He goes on, "the Model T Ford, A&P grocery stores, Twentieth Century-Fox, and WXYZ's weekly *Lone Ranger*" caused "cultural integration (some said degeneration)" (x). He writes that the "consumer culture . . . condoned hedonism and challenged . . . the work ethic" and "heightened for many the old question about personal identity and spiritual integrity in a society where the market appeared to structure and dominate human relationships" (x).

Such a consumer culture "transformed decisively the meaning of opportunity and success in American society, which for generations had stressed the importance of independent proprietorship" (Parrish xi), or, the American Dream. At the same time, Americans were drawn into "the problems of a larger world they increasingly influenced by their economic power and example" (xi) as they had been drawn into World War I. And the effects of that war led to a modernist attitude. During the Progressive era, Americans grew tired of "crusades . . . great deeds and heroic sacrifice" (3) and wanted to return to "normalcy" and moderation (9). Women gained the right to vote (9), and the foundation of a "utility empire" encouraged "efficiency and growth" in industry (35).

World War I "annihilated all reason, virtue, and human compassion. Italians turned on Italians; soldiers murdered innocent civilians; the machinery of violence killed and maimed indiscriminately" (Parrish 187). Those "left behind" expressed "rage," and the younger generation blamed the elder. Parrish writes, "Language itself. . . had been debased and could not be trusted" (187-88). Most American writers "saw the war as an unmitigated disaster" (188). A "collection of essays entitled *Civilization in the United States* . . . offered variations on an old theme played by Henry James: America did not have a civilization worthy of the name and what it did have remained indifferent to or destructive to the artistic spirit" (191). In it, Harold Stearns wrote, "'We have no heritage or tradition to which to cling except those that have already withered in our hands and turned to dust'" (qtd. in Parrish 191). These essayists "told the younger generation of American writers that it was absurd to think their efforts could change a spiritually impoverished society" (191). "In much of the fiction of the twenties, society became the enemy of personal fulfillment, the nemesis of the authentic self," writes Parrish, as "society constructed and manipulated" the roles that protagonists could play (192). Fictional heroes had only "small victories that preserved individual autonomy, dignity, and self-respect" (192); when they pursued "a single dream," they fell into "catastrophe" (193).

The "post-war generation of intellectuals" made Henry Adams, although he had died during the war, "a posthumous member of the lost generation" because they had re-discovered his *The Education of Henry Adams* (Parrish 194), in which he wrote that

> the exercise of political power in democratic society had become wholly divorced from intellectual and cultural sensibilities. Critical thinking was, in fact, a positive obstacle to political success. Intellectuals would remain marginal and isolated from the real sources of authority. Adams also questioned modern notions of social evolution and progress . . . . Finally, science and technology, symbolized by the electric dynamo, had put extraordinary power into human hands. But without a force such as the religion that once bound medieval communities together, this new energy would fuel only individual greed and social disintegration. (194)

Joseph Wood Krutch wrote that because science has decentered humans "from the center of the cosmology to the margins," it "grows more and more likely that he [man] must remain an ethical animal in a universe which contains no ethical element'" (qtd. in Parrish 195), indicating the influence of naturalism. In the naturalist view of the world, humans are colonized by science, being unable to trust their unconscious and being slaves to their animal natures. Walter Lippman wrote that there were no new values to replace the scientifically dashed old ones (qtd. in Parrish 196). We find evidence of this in Sherwood Anderson's dispossessed characters in *Winesburg, Ohio.* In 1926, H. L. Mencken "pronounced America unfit for serious artistic endeavors," according to Parrish (198). When Sacco and Vanzetti were executed in 1927 for a purported burglary, many writers despaired, and John Dos Passos wrote, "'we are two nations'" (qtd. in Parrish 203). According to Parrish, "The case defined political boundaries in America between left and right for many years to come . . . [and] generated a renewed sense of purpose and fraternity among American intellectuals" (203).

Under Herbert Hoover, scientific management becomes bureaucracy (Parrish 240), and we can easily see the situation in Frank Norris's "A Deal in Wheat" in Parrish's explanation of subsequent farm price fixing (246-47). Parrish writes that standardization of products led to homogenization of attitudes by way of "manufacturers, advertisers, the airwaves, and the silver screen" (x). And as the United States entered the Great War in 1917, it was not only an international force, but it also took center stage in world affairs, becoming a world leader by entering World War I and causing a decisive victory (Parrish xi). Effectively, the former colony had moved from the margin to the center in the world.

Between the Wars

As the Great War ended, great disillusionment set in. Far from perfecting ourselves as society gained knowledge and invented technology, we instead could see the vast waste that our new technologies had brought about. Modern advances in technology had only given us newer and more efficient ways to kill. This kind of disillusion had profound effects on literature, as authors thought that old literary forms were inadequate to express the new world; instead, they invented their own, new literary forms.

The decade of the 1940s encompassed "suburbanization, communist hysteria, atomic fear" (Foertsch 201). Two reasons Jacqueline Foertsch gives for the move of the white middle class to the suburbs is "their understandable fear of atomic attack on concentrated urban centres at the start of the cold war and their irrational fear of non-white urban neighbors" (189). However, these phenomena came about after the war had been won. The main event in 1940s America was the war. The United States had earlier declined to go to war against Hitler in Europe, but its isolationist stance was dramatically altered after Pearl Harbor was attacked by the Japanese on a Sunday in December 1941. United States citizens were so outraged that thousands volunteered for the military the very next day.

Their outrage led to a kind of national unity in which everyone supported the war effort. This feeling of unity, however, excluded those Japanese Americans on the West Coast, who were rounded up and detained in camps designed to prevent their communicating with the Japanese military, effectively marginalizing the Japanese Americans.

Conversely, other Asians gained a great opportunity to step out of their "Chinatown economy" (Foertsch 12) and join other Americans in manufacturing war matériel. Other disenfranchised groups of Americans, people of color, middle-class white women, and poor whites, were accepted into the war effort and thus gained an equality that they had not previously experienced. As well, people of color in the military distinguished themselves in battle, so well that the armed services were eventually desegregated.

White women and people of color rose to the national emergency of the Second World War to stand in for the men who had gone off to fight the war; however, their employment and brief stint of equality was abruptly terminated as the veterans returned and demanded their jobs back. Those who wanted to maintain their wartime employment came under immense pressure from various quarters to give it up. J. Edgar Hoover blamed working mothers for the crime in the country (Foertsch 29). Women were blamed for working for less pay than men, and Philip Wylie's *A Generation of Vipers* laid the blame for the growing consumerism in the United States at the feet of women, even though it was the "women who were manipulated by such obsessions—generated by men themselves—in an effort to return them acquiescently to house-keeping and child-raising" (29). Women's magazines joined the call for women to return home through the advertisements that they published, and propaganda by the government itself was instrumental in "the massive layoffs of female employees after the war" (Foertsch 29).

Critical trends in fiction and journalism were based on the philosophy of existentialism, which originated mostly in France, and the theory of New Criticism, both of which were inward-turning. Existentialism stresses the burden of freedom and the subsequent responsibility to self and others, the solitude of the individual, the absurdity of the lived existence, reliance upon oneself, and taking responsibility for oneself. Saul Bellow's first novel, *The Dangling Man* (1944) was regarded by critic Malcolm Bradbury and sociologist Frederick R. Karl as "a watershed novel" (Foertsch 34) because it presented the protagonist as existentialist. His existentialism is portrayed by his retreating into himself, which "defines the act of existential self-discovery" (Foertsch 34).

New Criticism is "an inward-turning interpretive method in its own right that, like the existentialist novelists it analysed, de-emphasised the historical and biographical aspects of a work's origins to focus exclusively (and some would say ultra-conservatively) on the work itself" (Foertsch 34). Because the New Critics were writers themselves and were "ensconced" in institutions of higher learning, English departments became makers of literary tastes. As well, these concepts can be found in "African American canonical works [, which] present an existential hero from a specifically black perspective, and white Southern novels [, which] focus on race, class, and sexual identity in essential ways" (35).

Foertsch claims that Americans can remember only the first half of the 1940s because in the second half, many of the momentous happenings of the late 1940s—"reconstruction of Europe, dividing . . . world spoils, and the formation of the present-day crisis in the Middle East"—happened "outside United States borders" and "lack[ed] the popular narrative (we might even say the Hollywood treatment) that would have established them in American memory" (201).

Post-World War II

In the Introduction to his *The Proud Decades: America in War and Peace, 1941-1960*, John Patrick Diggins lists the themes of the period: "the cold war . . . [,] domestic politics . . . [,] the changing nature of American society . . . [,] popular culture and the enduring idols of Americans young and old; higher culture and the influence of European refugee intellectuals; and the early civil rights movement and the first stirrings of feminism" (xiii). Diggins apparently does not associate the women's suffrage movement with feminism, but he does mention as an example of the "variety and ambiguity" of the period "the tension . . . between the mood of moderation in national politics and the daring innovation that exploded in cultural modernism" (xiv).

Frederick R. Karl sees the decade of the 1950s as "ambiguous" (20) and points out the many ways "the decade itself was a forgery" (21). He notes that the 1950s was "demarcated on one side by the end of the war and on the other by the uproar of the sixties" (20). He points out that 50,000 Americans died in the "forgotten" Korean War (21) and states that contemporary memory of the 1950s is based on myth and deceit. McCarthyism and the Cold War brought about a great deal of paranoia. Instead of seeing the fifties as "the victory of American culture and values over those of its closest rival, the Soviet Union" (20), Karl suggests that we are overlooking much of the deceit of the decade and uses the rigged television quiz show *Twenty-One* as an example. Karl writes that the contestants "became performers," and the show itself "became part of the selling of America in the fifties, part of the commodification of information and the reliance on appearances" (25). He writes that the situation of the show mirrored the "Cold War in miniature" (26) in its "reliance on superficial knowledge and its need to recreate reality, to rely on performance over even superficial information" (27). Meanwhile, the "political emphasis on national survival and American exclusionism became transformed into literary terms of counterfeiting and invisibility" (24). In regard to literature, Karl highlights that "the difficulty of self-identification in a counterfeit or imitational context becomes apparent in several of the novels in the earlier part of the decade" (32). Karl sees this motif in Ellison's *Invisible Man,* Bellow's *Augie March,* and Baldwin's *Go Tell It on the Mountain.*

Karl expands his discussion to include the significant rearrangement of population and shifts his attention to the rebellion in the 1950s. He states, "It was becoming clear by the fifties that the culture was stacked against the so-called 'people'" (36); however, "everything depended on keeping a public united in the Cold War" (37). In this respect, each field tries to keep itself united: Elvis Presley blends musical forms and times, and the mass media present a vision of united Americans.

But "as elements in the fifties culture clashed" (Karl 44), it is necessary to identify what was occurring. At this point, two fictions, *Naked Lunch* and *Peyton Place,* "exemplify how elements we associate with the sixties were already surging in the fifties" (44). Karl writes that Jack Kerouac's *On the Road* and J. D. Salinger's *The Catcher in the Rye* both demonstrated as well that not every American was content. Taken together, these novels indicate a deep cultural split in the United States.

Karl pays attention to some specific voices in the 1960s. Walker Percy, John Hawkes, Flannery O'Connor, William Styron, Norman Mailer, John Updike, and Bernard Malamud all search for something authentic from different perspectives. Karl writes: "the play between high and low culture, or midcult, was, in several respects, the pull and tear of the decade's dichotomies that at most levels resisted all efforts at resolution . . . . Against such pressures was a counter-movement which represented a more open, democratic force that blasted through in the mid-to-late sixties" (59).

Josephine G. Hendin writes that the postwar culture of the United States "forged dynamic new fusions and combinations" (1). Hendin highlights the variety of postwar American writing and suggests that "the enduring American gift may be precisely that constant process of exchange and incorporation that brings about a repositioning of the center" (2). Hendin emphasizes that rebellion and despair dominate postwar American writing. But rather than lingering over divisions, Hendin stresses the creative energy that conflict evokes and states that "new social arrangements provoked a new aesthetic openness" (7).

Additionally, the interaction between margin and mainstream nourished the acceptance of new voices. As one of the most distinct voices, African American literature plays an important role. Similarly, "the growth and prominence of ethnic literatures are one of the remarkable features of postwar American writing" (Hendin 9). Hendin writes that conflict itself has contributed to the growth and development of Asian American, Hispanic American, and Native American literature" (11) and emphasizes that African American studies is "a model that has inspired the growth of ethnic studies in general" (9) in this country, in the same way that Ashcroft, Griffith, and Tiffin suggest that American literature is a model for other postcolonial literatures.

Martin Halliwell writes that one must understand "cold war ideology" and the "tangible effects on middle-class life" from the "economic prosperity that began in World War II" in order to understand the 1950s culture. No one questioned "political decisions that contributed to the nation's rise to eminence"; instead, the "mass media encouraged consumers to simply enjoy the material comforts that international prestige brought" (2). He writes that the change occurred "from inward-looking conservatism of the 1950s to the political activism of the mid-1960s" (3). He sees that "recent cultural historians . . . focus on 1950s culture as a site of dualities, tensions and contradictions" (3). Halliwell points out that, though "'One nation under God' [was] added to the Pledge of Allegiance in 1954," this decade "was vilified in the 1960s" (4).

Some of the paradoxes that he points out are "'optimism along with the gnawing fear of doomsday bombs, . . . great poverty in the midst of unprecedented prosperity, and . . . flowery rhetoric about equality along with the practice of rampant racism and sexism'" (Ronald Oakley qtd. in Halliwell 4). He states that "the decade was one of the defining periods of the twentieth century, prefiguring the materialism of the 1980s, the media control of the 1990s, and the ascendancy of the Right in the early twenty-first century" (4). He focuses on "four primary frames of reference–culture, ideas, spaces and identities" to show how they "were all contested in the 1950s, with the view that the decade is best characterized as a struggle between conflicting forces . . . . economic, ideological political, cultural and experiential" (11-12). "Forces of standardization," he writes, like the Billboard Top 40, television sitcoms, and suburban life, "came into contact with cultures of hybridity" like rock and roll music (242) and, of course, the civil rights movement.

While some writers of the 1950s were seen as rebels, Halliwell points out that "the climate of censorship made it difficult for writers to offer direct social commentary" (53), referring to the idea of containment—containing not just the Communists, but also containing the citizenry (8). As Senator Joseph McCarthy sought to eliminate the Communists that he claimed had infiltrated the United States government, he effectively contained the citizens; everyone was afraid of being branded unpatriotic. Halliwell quotes Morris Dickstein about "cultural consensus": the 1950s was "'a moment when outsiders were becoming insiders, when American literature . . . was becoming decentred, or multicentred, feeding on new energies from the periphery'" (53). Until *Brown v. Board of Education* in 1954, Halliwell writes, there was "inevitable" exile, "either internal or external," for African American writers. There was a "climate of distrust during the McCarthy and [Julius and Ethel] Rosenberg years" (243).

Leerom Medovoi's *Rebels: Youth and the Cold War Origins of Identity* is a social, historical, cultural, and literary study on the very concepts of "identity" and "rebellion." Medovoi places his study of "identity" and "rebellion" in the context of Cold War America, and by doing so, he explicitly engages in the analysis of American film, literature, music, and pop culture, in the frame of a developing identity-obsessed generation. The first chapter links identitarian thought and the Cold War world. On the basis of the origin of "identity" and the invention of this concept by Erik Erikson, Medovoi turns to a historical explanation: the form of a triangulated rivalry of three worlds and the mode of mass consumption and production. Taken together, "postwar American culture was deeply troubled by ideological tension between the norms of Fordist suburbia and the America idealized by the three worlds imaginary" (22), or the first, second, and third world economies. Building his study on this assertion, Medovoi takes Cold War "youth" and "the teenager" into account and examines how the concepts of "identity" and "rebellion" became rapidly appealing. He analyzes the "celebration of rebellion as an American ideal by the public arbiters of Cold War culture" (55) and explicates the "identitarianization of American literature" (56). Medovoi emphasizes that "where the old canon had emphasized the development of American literary realism, the new canon placed at its apex the word of the so-called American Renaissance" (58). In the process, literary criticism makes use of the allegory of development, especially the rebel allegory.

Finally, Medovoi shows how "identity criticism," the "identity novel," integrated "identity canons," and "rebel allegories" (85) relate to the image and ideas of rebellion in the context of pop culture—rock and roll, for example. Through the imaginary processes, he writes, the "youth audience began to identify with 'identity,' viewing themselves as emergent personalities entitled to rebel against suburban conformity in the name of their own sovereign self-definition against adults" (92). Two films, *Rebel without a Cause* and *King Creole,* popularized this notion. Medovoi considers Oedipal dramas of the suburban family, tracing a narrative pattern in which identity emerges through a rebellious son's struggle against an impotent father who lacks the capacity for autonomous self-assertion. He examines the political complexities of the bad boy's gender dynamics on the level of a fraternal public. By looking at the constitutive bonds of the bad-boy gangs celebrated in key contexts by the Beat generation writers, Medovoi explores the collectivization of young rebel identity. Using Kerouac's *On the Road* as a backdrop to the concept of identity in the 1950s, Medovoi states that "what the beat texts succeeded in doing was to lay claim on the identity narrative of fifties youth culture, and to name its audience the 'beat generation'" (217). The public discourse surrounding the Beat generation "converged in the image of an age group that clashes with mainstream America" (222). Medovoi's statement emphasizes the homosocial aspects of the relationships of both the literary characters and real personas of the Beats—the Beat writers effectively used their "fictionalized autobiography" to advance their claims (223). Thus their characters' lives follow the authors' lives. Two outstanding examples of this phenomenon are Kerouac's *On the Road* and John Clellon Holmes's *Go!* In addition to a boy gang, "feminist representations of male power were paternalized in the process" (258). The female rebel appears as the sexual bad girl and the tomboy. He writes that rebel girls "actually played a much larger role in imaginative postwar American culture" than may have been realized at the time (266).

The Rebellious Sixties and the Copacetic Seventies

At some point, margins may become the center; for instance, the 1960s. This was a decade which saw several important struggles: the civil rights movement, the Vietnam War, the war on poverty, and the space race. A theme of Sharon Monteith's *American Culture in the 1960s* is that local and regional events contribute to the national image, or that margins contribute to center. She writes that "what was often seen as marginal or socially peripheral can prove symbolically central to the cultural shifts of the 1960s" (3). The movement for civil rights for African Americans, protests against the war in Vietnam, fear of a nuclear disaster, a growing concern with the environment, and a call for rights for women and homosexuals were all coming from the margins of society; the rebellion was against the hegemony that had condoned Jim Crow practices, had sent the young of the poor off to war, was facing the Soviets down with nuclear weapons, and was oppressing women and homosexuals. These issues from the margin became part of the cultural shifts. Here the rebellious counterculture can be seen as the colonized revolting against the colonizer.

However, critique was initiated not only by the disenfranchised but also by established intellectuals. Margin becomes center and local becomes national when several white Birmingham clergymen write an open letter, "A Call For Unity," to Martin Luther King, Jr. locally, only to have him respond nationally in "Letter from Birmingham Jail" (Monteith 2). Another example is that Wendell Berry's local view, considered marginal, of environmental concerns through his fiction becomes national news through Rachel Carson's *Silent Spring*. Monteith writes that he "repeatedly stated that the view from his window on the South encompassed not only the nation but also the world" (3).

John F. Kennedy's assassination brought about a loss of innocence for America, a loss of hope that change could be brought about. His utopian image and frontier analogies had excited many young people with the hope that they could actually effect change (Monteith 18). The Beats had an influence on the counterculture through Ginsberg's "Howl," Kerouac's Dean Moriarty (8), and the "romance of being 'on the road'" (41).

There were tensions between democratic ideals and undemocratic practices (Monteith 6), between the public and the private (7). In personal memory, local events supersede national events, but can actually encompass the nation; Monteith writes that the participants gave themselves a role in history, but that our collective memory may not be accurate because this is when the media began to interpret events, and there may have been a "cultural production" of memories (188). According to Monteith, this was "the moment just before conglomerates controlled all mass cultural forms" (1). Media events were created by the media, which immediately began archiving the images, "packaging news as history" (29), and "shaping collective memories" (28). The media were instrumental in shaping John Glenn's 1962 flight, President Kennedy's funeral coverage, and the 1969 moon landing (29). Public spectacle became public statement. The power of the media was such that their images became our culture (153).

Sharon Monteith writes that "a culture can be most expressive at its boundaries" (4). She points out that, even before desegregation laws were passed, rock and roll "music [had] integrated audiences" (39). Andy Warhol made celebrity a commodity, and famously declared that everyone would have "15 minutes of fame" (38). Comics making their jokes about the events in the country caused "humour [to become] social indictment" (57). The "principles and strategies" of the civil rights movement "were revised to fit other political platforms" like rights for Native Americans, women, gays, and the environment and protests against the war (151). James Conaway has stated that the hegemony of the time was like "the monarch whose omnipotence comes by virtue of age and masculinity and not much else, a false entitlement shared by Dad's entire generation that would be swept away in an angry social tide" (qtd. in Monteith 191). This feeling of entitlement is demonstrated in the smugness of the 1950s that the protagonist resists in Phillip Roth's *Good-bye, Columbus*.

But by 1982, "the 'Woodstock Nation' was declared to have finally and quietly transformed middle America" (Monteith 5), and the music of the counterculture was later used to sell products, used as Muzak in elevators (34). By the end of the twentieth century, those who had occupied the margins in the 1960s had "often entered the mainstream" (201). The margin had become the center.

The years 1960 through 1974 were marked at either end by the election of John F. Kennedy and the resignation of Richard M. Nixon. During those years whether and how to use the federal government became the underlying issue of political division and political posturing (Blum 476). This was a time period in which many thoughtful persons wanted to see the federal government assist in bringing about some social justice for the outsiders: the racial minorities, women, the poor.

Some notable events and situations during the time were Kennedy's New Frontier and Lyndon Baines Johnson's Great Society, the Cold War with its arms and technology race with the Soviet Union, the burgeoning consumer culture, the rise in power of the military-industrial complex, the Vietnam War with its anti-war protesters, segregation and the civil rights movement, and a widening gap between the haves and the have-nots, with the haves' affluence growing and the have-nots' poverty unrelenting. There was private wealth and public squalor (Blum 13). There was no apparent national purpose, so three formal investigations were launched to discern a national purpose (11-12).

Kennedy urged the end of colonialism even as he condoned the involvement of the United States in the affairs of Vietnam (Blum 18) and retained "alliances with European colonial powers" (7). He wanted to use American resources to support developing nations in Africa, Asia, and Central America (18), even though he opposed Soviet expansion (4).

A series of unauthorized wars began in the 1960s: Kennedy's Bay of Pigs, Kennedy's, Johnson's, and Nixon's Vietnam. Gerald Ford struck back at Cambodia, and in 1979 Jimmy Carter authorized a military action to rescue American hostages from Iran (Blum 478). During this time, Congress attempted to rein in the powers of the executive branch, but had little success: even though they passed the War Powers Act of 1974 (477), they continued to fund the war in Vietnam and could do nothing about the presidential veto (478). Presidents continued to act without congressional authority (477), including Reagan's 1983 invasion of Grenada.

The New Frontier led to the first man on the moon in 1969. The Great Society was unable to wipe out poverty. Using resources for the Vietnam War allowed fewer resources for lifting up the poor (Blum 479). Both the CIA and the FBI engaged in illegal activities to further the political agendas of the executive branch, exposed by Congress in hearings in 1975 and 1976 (478). Social protest lost its momentum because it was fragmented (480). Peaceful protests against the war and for civil rights turned violent. The war in Vietnam was lost in 1975, and the minority groups, as they gained a voice in affairs, became conventional and "flowed into the political mainstream" (480).

During his second term in office Nixon backed away from any constructive use of the federal government, and this position "continued, accelerating during the 1980s" (Blum 480-81). During this time industry and finance were deregulated and taxes were reduced on "corporations and wealthy Americans" (481), and by 1990, the nation had returned to its 1960 situation of great gaps in wealth and privilege between classes of its citizens. The "liberal aspirations of that creative time" (481) needed to be revived.

The Affluent Eighties and the Greedy Nineties

Graham Thompson writes that the recovery of "marginalized histories and texts redefined the very notion of what constituted a national culture" (2). But, he writes, Reaganomics "shape[d] the decade" of the 1980s, which was "enabled" by "the moral and social conservatism of voters—around issues such as abortion, crime and patriotism" (10). Reaganomics was called "voodoo economics" by George H. W. Bush before Bush became Reagan's running mate in the 1980 presidential election, and it was a response to "stagflation," which was "a combination of rising inflation and economic stagnation" (7) with high unemployment, high levels of "government spending, high interest rates," with both "increasing wages and increasing prices" which "threatened to undermine the prosperity of the 1950s and 60s" (7).

Because Reaganomics favored corporations and investors, the consumers from the 1950s were transformed into investors in the 1980s, as economic policy was "focused not on stimulating demand but on stimulating investment and consumption," since the policies provided "incentives for wealth creation" among the citizens (Thompson 8). According to Thompson, these economic policies "emphasized regeneration and reinvention . . . . [which made] Reaganomics . . . not just an economic vision but a moral vision too," and the policies allowed both "Republicans and Democrats to enjoy the best of political worlds" (8). Activity on Wall Street reflected the investor attitude, as "Not only did the level of trading increase, but also a whole wave of mergers and acquisitions" (11). The Reagan administration was "reluctan[t] . . . to enforce antitrust laws," and "notorious forms of financing emerged" (11).

Thompson stresses the "historical importance of surveillance and self-surveillance in American culture" (2). He states that Reagan was a "character who stands in for America" for the whole decade, as that decade "stand[s] in for the entire postwar period of American history" (3). According to Michael Rogin,

whom Thompson quotes, Reagan "'merged his on- and off-screen identities',"
which effectively reflected the breakdown of oppositions "'between surface and
depth, the authentic and the inauthentic, the imaginary and the real, signifier and
signified'," and Thompson goes on to write that "the distinctions between history
and fiction [became] increasingly tenuous" (4). Thompson points out that the
"eighties culture [was] driven, and dominated, by the production and circulation
of the image" (5) and that "the boundaries between fact and fiction, image and
identity . . . blurred to the point of collapse" (5).

The culture wars of the 1980s was a "battle over social and cultural power
between those on the left and the right" stimulated by "the social conservative
backlash against the 1960s," which "was every bit as important an element in
Reaganomics as was the supply-side economics aimed at turning round the
American economy" (Thompson 9).

The 1980s saw the emergence of "yuppies," who were interested in
"wealth, . . . expensive branded products . . . consumer technology . . . [and
whose] lifestyles revolv[ed] around drinking, eating, shopping, fashion, and body-
sculpting" (Thompson 12). New consumer technology included the cellular phone
and the VCR. Tom Wolfe and other writers "disparag[ed] the New York yuppie
culture," while Oliver Stone showed on film "the quick-moving and predatory
nature of financial capital in the 1980s and tried to show the damaging impact on
the jobs and lives of the people who worked for companies at the heart of the
mergers and acquisitions frenzy" (13). But "by the end of the 1980s, the
fraudulent acquisition of what many considered to be obscene amounts of money
helped temper the decade of greed," which had been assisted by the "advent of
computerized trading" which "facilitated" a "truly globalized trading
environment" (14).

The United States "carved out new markets in areas in which it would
become a world leader" in video games and other computer software (Thompson
29), but the United States had very little to do with the "technology behind the
video recorder and the video tape, the digital compact disc and portable music

players" (180). A "series of scandals[,] . . . insider trading and fraud on Wall Street, the Iran-Contra affair, the televangelists" indicated a mood of "doubt and mistrust" (181). Thompson quotes Paul Giles regarding "the declining hegemony of the United States" (181). In a section of *American Culture in the 1980s* called "Transatlantic Circulations," Thompson looks back and points out the "reluctance on the part of British cultural elites to acknowledge U. S. culture" in the nineteenth century and "a corresponding desire from some Americans to self-consciously produce a national literary culture worthy of attention" (160). He states that "in 1916, Randolph Bourne was still complaining vehemently about English influence" (160); Bourne states that "the ruling class of Anglo-Saxon descendants in these American States" cling to "English snobberies, English religion, English literary styles, English literary reverences and canons; English ethics, English superiorities" and that the "distinctively American spirit . . . has had to exist on sufferance alongside of this other cult, unconsciously belittled by our cultural makers of opinion" (qtd. in Thompson 161).

Haynes Johnson, a Pulitzer Prize-winning journalist, in *Sleepwalking Through History: America in the Reagan Years,* shows how in "the Reagan decade . . . America fell from dominant world power to struggling debtor nation and optimism turned to foreboding. . . . [The] era [was] nurtured by greed and a morality that found virtue in not getting caught" (back cover). The "attitudes that typified America during the eighties and nineties" were "reckless, self-indulgent," and "continue to influence how we respond to foreign and domestic events" (463). The title itself says a great deal: while Americans slept, greedy capitalists walked off with all of the assets. Johnson writes that Reagan's "ideological cheerleading provided . . . a 'new theology of capitalism'" (467).

Johnson points out three trends of the 1980s which "are essential to understanding what came next": one is "metaphysical" (469), the second is the growth in power of the news media, and the third "involved ideology, both political and economic" (472). The metaphysical trend "involve[ed] the national spirit . . . . And it was here that Ronald Reagan played so great a role" (469).

With his "reassuring presence, his evocation of patriotic myths and fables, [he] powerfully allayed the doubts and divisions that were the legacies of such cynicism-producing disasters as Vietnam and Watergate. . . . Reagan made Americans feel good again" (469). He would not have won the presidency without the disaster surrounding the United States' hostages in Iran, but as the Iranians released the hostages on the day of his inauguration in 1981, the country felt "a lift it never lost during his presidency" (470). And Reagan associated himself with the "disintegration of the Soviet Union and the outbreak of democracy worldwide," making Americans think of themselves as "history's winners" (469). Johnson points out that this "sense of invulnerability was an illusion," and that "radical Islamic fundamentalism . . . marked the Reagan years and those of his three presidential successors, George H. W. Bush, Bill Clinton, and George W. Bush" dating the "age of terror . . . from that Iranian revolution" (470).

Along with "the growth of a high-tech revolution and the Internet," cable television with its "around-the-clock deregulated cable news . . . . formed a power too often put to ignoble uses," according to Johnson. He points out that all of "the new media" had to struggle for a share of "fragmented markets, struggling to capture the attention of a public diverted by the lure of get-rich-quick dreams and tuning out of serious presentation of issues," and this was the beginning of their presentation of "news events with the widest popular appeal . . . . a constant offering of all-scandal, all-celebrity, all-spectacle" events like the O. J. Simpson trial, the Monica Lewinsky affair, and the death of Princess Diana (Johnson 470).

The trend involving political and economic ideology "represented the crest of the American conservative movement that began with Barry Goldwater in 1964 and reached its apogee in the eighties" (Johnson 472). The "ideological forces that coalesced with Ronald Reagan's beliefs . . . continued to exert a profound influence on America's attitudes, its policies, its politics, its government, and its economy—and remain fixtures of national life today" (472). The two important challenges in what Johnson calls "the new age of terror" are gaining "greater security" without taking away the freedom and liberty that are "democratic bedrock principles" and "restoring public faith in the capitalistic system" (473).

According to Howard Zinn, three successive presidents, Carter, Reagan, and Bush, were all cultural manipulators in making income tax less progressive and Social Security tax more regressive; he writes that "three-fourths of all wage earners paid more each year through the Social Security tax than through the income tax" (Zinn 350). By the end of the Reagan administration, the wealth gap had dramatically widened between the rich and the poor. The word *welfare* was made even worse by its "constant derogatory use" (349), even though, he points out, the word was never attached to the handouts to corporations.

Reagan ignored a law passed by Congress against supporting the Iran contras, maintaining "plausible denial," and neither he nor Oliver North, who was convicted of lying to Congress regarding the situation, went to jail. Reagan allowed no media representatives to observe the invasion of Grenada. Reagan more than quadrupled United States' aid to El Salvador; when an embarrassed Congress tried to tie United States aid to "progress in human rights," Reagan scoffed and "certified" himself that the progress was being made (Zinn 362). Terrorism is defined by Stephen Shalom as "politically motivated violence perpetrated against non-combatant targets" (qtd. in Zinn 363) and "the U. S. raid on Libya" fit the definition (363). The Reagan years were rife with discontent: teachers' strikes, foreclosures, the unemployed. Handicapped people organized to get the Americans with Disabilities Act passed; protesters against honoring accused genocidist Christopher Columbus got the American Indians behind them and eventually the National Council of Churches, to "refrain from celebrating" Columbus Day (407). These are examples of the agitation that Zinn, a historian and social activist, recommends in his *A People's History of the United States*. Other examples: protests against the Vietnam War, the grape boycott of the sixties.

According to Zinn, the middle class provides the buffer between the upper and lower classes. The "Establishment" continues to dole out "small rewards" for the "obedience and loyalty of millions" of middle-class workers who maintain the system (Zinn 418). The leaders "distribute just enough wealth to just enough people to limit discontent to a troublesome minority" (414), leaving the rest to share the leftovers.

In Zinn's view, the Clinton presidency was characterized by "caution and conservatism" and a "subservience to big business" (Zinn 426). The 1996 "Crime Bill" established or extended a policy of punishment rather than prevention. Zinn quotes H. L. Mencken to aver that the government must "keep the populace alarmed by menacing it with an endless series of hobgoblins, all of them imaginary" (429). He writes that Clinton joined the Republicans in fighting "big government," which meant "social services" (433). Zinn points out that there were no complaints against big government until the government "passed social legislation for the poor" (436). He writes that Clinton also maintained the military as the Republicans wanted and "overlooked human rights violations . . . for the sake of commerce" (442). There was increasing diversity in the country, even as racism remained. There were attempts to organize the discontent among the African Americans with the "Rainbow Coalition" and "The Million Man March," and labor unions were re-energized (457).

In the 2000 election, Zinn writes, both parties were much alike, but Bush was favored by the corporations, the holders of money. As far as the "war on terrorism," the Patriot Act combined patriotism with revenge, he avers, and allowed the George W. Bush government to hold even American citizens without lawyers, without hearing, and without charges at Guantanamo Bay, Cuba, and other, secret, locations.

Zinn concludes by reverting to the Declaration of Independence's statements that "government was secondary, that the people who established it were primary" (475). He recommends that the common man must be more active in the affairs of the state. The future of democracy, he writes, "depend[s] on the people, and their growing consciousness of what [is] the decent way to relate to their fellow human beings all over the world" (475).

CHAPTER FIVE: MINORITY STRUGGLES TO BECOME AMERICAN

*. . . minority discourses in America . . . remain at a stage where the anxiety of
identity formation is paramount.*
—Henry Louis Gates, Jr.

Marginalized Groups

One practice of deconstruction is especially relevant in locating characters
from minority groups in American fiction. Deconstructionist thinkers deny the
use of either-or without the corresponding neither-nor and both-and.
Deconstruction looks at binary oppositions that we usually never question, such as
the opposition of male and female, inside and outside, up and down, and so forth,
with a corresponding value that one is more desirable than the other. In this
approach, we can valorize that which is devalued in the literature and devalue that
which is valorized in the literature to come up with some startling insights.
Paying particular attention to marginalized characters is just one way of
rethinking a story, and paying attention to marginalized groups in the United
States is one way of rethinking what it means to be American.

The 1980s and 1990s saw the greater publication of writers from
marginalized groups, allowing many readers to become more open-minded to the
life and culture of someone from a different ethnicity. But at the same time,
several new writers from ethnic minorities garnered negative attention from their
native people, some of whom felt they were "sellouts" to their culture and
heritage. By the late twentieth century, there was a need for a new critical
consciousness; the study of literature had completely changed since the 1950s.

Literary study by historians "led to the broader purpose of humanizing future generations," but cultural critics see that literary works now participate in "a conversation with several discourses—popular, economic, social, material" (Hutner vii), and, we might add, political. Gordon Hutner writes that the cultural debate about expanding the American literary canon that was carried on in the 1980s and 1990s "had been going on at least since the 1950s," as the "new critical consciousness revealed a generational split" (vi).

Through social history we can locate the relationships of seven of the marginalized groups to both the minority and the majority cultures, as well as understand the necessity for self-transformation, using a literary example to represent each of the groups.

Native Americans

In the field of Native American literature the label of "Native American literature" is unacceptable to some. According to Michael Dorris, in his "Native American Literature in an Ethnohistorical Context," "English literature is expected to be *in* English, and to be therefore accessible first and foremost to English-speaking clients" (147). He states that "the writings in English by Native people and about 'Native' themes" are different from the traditional literatures because "they were originally composed in a foreign language (English), and their intended audience is primarily Euro-American and not tribal" (153). He writes that it is impossible "to subsume the extraordinarily large and diverse corpora of traditional Native American oral literatures under the single rubric of 'Indian literature'," and that "the term 'American Indian Literature' is largely ambiguous and begs more questions than it answers" (149). Dorris states that Native American cultures are "fragile, regressive, deteriorating entities, teetering on the brink of extinction" (153) and that the stereotype of Native Americans cannot possibly convey Native Americans' ideas. Dorris writes that "Native American societies are not one-dimensional and fixed on days gone by" (155), as the stereotype represents, and concludes that the investigation into Native American literature is not an easy task but calls for multi-dimensional efforts.

In *Other Destinies: Understanding the American Indian Novel*, Louis Owens writes that "Before 1968 only nine novels by American Indian authors had been published" (24). However, he writes that, when Scott Momaday published *House Made of Dawn* in 1968 and *The Way to Rainy Mountain* in 1969, it was "as if Momaday had triggered a long-dormant need among Indian writers, [and] the 1970s saw the publication of a stream of novels by Indian authors" and lists twelve of these writers, including James Welch, Gerald Vizenor, and Leslie Marmon Silko. He continues that in the 1980s and 1990s the works of eight other Indian authors were published, including works by Louise Erdrich, Paula Gunn Allen, and himself. As well, during that time Momaday, Vizenor, and Welch published new works (24). In two decades, then, twenty American Indian authors were published, ushering in a new era for Native authors.

Evolution in Writing

Owens writes that the tone and attitude of Native American authors has undergone an evolution throughout the one hundred and fifty years of Native Americans' writing in English. They go from outrage to alienation to despair and finally to self-transformation. For example, Owens points out that "In the beginning, the mixedblood Cherokee author John Rollin Ridge felt obligated to disguise his outrage at America's genocidal treatment of his tribe, accomplishing this disguise by writing a novel masquerading as a biography of a California bandit"; then the portrayal of a mixedblood shows the "bitter sense of isolation and estrangement" in Mourning Dove's 1927 *Cogewea*, and Owens notes that this novel has an atmosphere that is "bittersweet, romantic," an "atmosphere that surrounds the Indian in much American literature" (24-25). However, he also notes that this sense of romance had started to dissipate from the Indian novel when Joseph Mathews and D'Arcy McNickle started to write. Mathews's 1934

Sundown, as its title suggests, is about the "nightmare time of new oil money and dissolution for the Osage" and is filled with "naturalistic despair" as the protagonist "slips into the deracinated no-Indian's-land between Osage and white worlds" (25). McNickle, too, has a naturalistic bent to his 1936 *The Surrounded*, and, again as suggested by the title, the protagonist "never has a chance within a civilization bent on turning Indians into Europeans" (25), just as, I contend, the European colonists had attempted to turn themselves into Americans.

Judith A. Antell agrees that, since the publication of N. Scott Momaday's *House Made of Dawn*, American Indian writings have attracted more and more attention. The novels of Momaday, James Welch, and Leslie Marmon Silko, she writes, "are extremely important not only for the literary accomplishments they represent, but also because through them we are able to hear the Indian voice which has so rarely been acknowledged" (213). In particular, they highlight the "the power and importance of the feminine principle" (213) and of male alienation.

Major themes of the twentieth-century American Indian novel are the "Indian people's alienation, cultural conflicts, sense of loss, and the shame of losing" (Antell 214). Antell indicates that these writers focus on the alienated men for several reasons: that the Indian men "may present the more 'tragic' figures in a dramatic sense . . . [and] provide the greater comfort to the dominant society, a comfort which comes from believing that Indians really have changed" (214).

More importantly, Momaday, Welch, and Silko use the alienated men to "address the power and significance of Indian women" (Antell 215). These writers are strongly aware of the fact that the power of Indian women comes from the traditional tribal context. Thus, a sense of belonging is of primary importance for Indian people. From this perspective, "estrangement is seen as so abnormal that narratives and rituals that restore the estranged to his or her place in the tribal matrix abound" (215).

A significant plot in three novels, Momaday's *House Made of Dawn*, Welch's *The Death of Jim Loney*, and Silko's *Ceremony*, is that men are separated from their mothers, who are the conveyors of culture. Yet the authors "separate these men from Indian women and the feminine principle, indicating that the feminine principle is their source of integration and connection" (Antell 217). Additionally, "the protagonists will eventually find their correct place in the universe of life, but not before they have knowingly participated in ancient rituals" (217). Antell states that the stories of alienated Indian men reveal "the stories of female power as acknowledged through ritual and ceremony" (220). Instead of constructing assimilationist solutions for the alienated men, these three writers use the form of ancient rituals, and the theme of ritual makes Indian novels distinct from white novels.

Starting with Momaday, who is, according to Owens, "the spiritual father of today's Native American writers," the American Indian protagonist, even though "alienated and fragmented" and unable to "articulate his identity as an Indian," can now come "full circle, back home to his Southwestern pueblo and a secure knowledge of who he is" (Owens 25). Momaday's novels show "a process of becoming, and demonstrates Bakhtin's contention that 'one's own discourse is gradually and slowly wrought out of others' words that have been acknowledged and assimilated'" (25).

Gerald Vizenor

Assimilation, or lack of it, is another major theme in novels by contemporary Native American writers, but even those who assimilate into the dominant culture express a sense of loss of the old ways. For example, in Gerald Vizenor's 1992 *Dead Voices*, Bagese Bear protects and celebrates the Native American culture that is left after the dominant white culture has encroached upon it. The shape of both the work itself and the "game" that it describes reflects the shape of a worldview held by many oral cultures: a cyclical, circular shape with an important center. Bagese Bear obviously considers the dominant culture to be inferior both morally and spiritually; the theme of the book is the loss suffered by the marginalized culture. The circular shape of time in the Native American world view brings the speaker closer to both the future and the past, but "the best . . . stories include experiences of the present" (50).

Bagese Bear's stories are important, especially in an oral tradition, which deals in truth and moral relationships. They are the exact opposite of the "dead voices" of the dominant culture, which include lectures, printed books, and poison. The oral stories exemplify a "natural" relationship between humans and the rest of the world; the dead voices of the "wordies" are separated from nature and cover up nature with chemicals: laundry products, insecticides.

Native American culture is based on the land, the tribe, and the past; each contributes to the sense of self and close relationship to the center. Native Americans are close to their names and their environment. They see the word as powerful and sacred and believe that they have a responsibility to use it properly. "Wordies" have no sense of relationship with the natural world nor with the sanctity of words, hence the title *Dead Voices*.

The game Bagese plays, the *wanaki* trickster game of natural meditation, is created by Stone as "his war with loneliness and with human separations from the natural world" (29). *Wanaki* means "a chance at peace" (17). Vizenor uses sarcasm, irony, and allegory to describe the results of the marginalization of the Native American culture. Sarcasm and irony abound in the book, but the story about the Fleas is an especially good allegory to show their relationship to the majority culture.

The Fleas, just as each of the other animals, come "down from the wild treelines to our tribal agonies in the cities." The exterminator, representing the dominant culture's genocidal policies, comes to eradicate the fleas with his chemicals, which are not in tune with nature. He spreads fear of fleas (Native Americans) to ensure his own survival in the "chemical civilization." The fleas are inspired to "a new consciousness and a counter movement," a self-transformation, and demand their "rights to the animals and birds on the block" (47).

African Americans

African American literature is a key genre in the field of literary studies in the twentieth and twenty-first centuries. Primary focuses have been on slave narratives, the Harlem Renaissance, the civil rights movement, and the Black Arts movement. Laban Carrick Hill's *Harlem Stomp! A Cultural History of the Harlem Renaissance,* Ira Katznelson's *When Affirmative Action Was White: An Untold History of Racial Inequality in Twentieth-Century America*, and James Edward Smethurst's *The Black Arts Movement* examine this history from the perspective of New Historicism. They attempt to uncover something beneath the mainstream studies and criticisms. Their studies of African American literature examine not only the re-establishment of African American literary tradition in the twentieth century, but also modernist and postmodernist elements in African American literature. In addition, the political aspects found in African American literature, like Left and Right, offer another point of current literary study.

Since 1920, the political Left of the dominant culture has had great influence on the African American culture, but there has been an "equally profound influence of African American culture on the Left" (Mullen and Smethurst 3). In their *Left of the Color Line: Race, Radicalism, and Twentieth-Century Literature of the United States,* Mullen and Smethurst state that the Left has opted for a life on the periphery, even though it has potential for great impact. But one continuity in the Left, they write, is a great "interest in race and ethnicity" (3).

When Alain Locke published *The New Negro* in 1925, adherents of three differing ideologies were vying for leadership of working-class black Americans, and all of them made great efforts to define the politics of the New Negro. The "important postwar ideological fight [was] between advocates of black nationalism, socialism, and American capitalism who in different ways struggled to position themselves as leaders" (Dawahare 68). Locke distanced himself from communism, though, and "appropriates the rhetoric of the Left and the black nationalists," maneuvering between the two because he advocated that "the New Negro possess a black 'national' identity and a patriotic loyalty to American capitalism that transcend class differences and interests" (68). Locke's book suggests that the New Negro might form only a small part of the black population and that the New Negro would be different from the "genuine radical," whose writings would have been excluded from Locke's book (68), indicating a different kind of relationship to the rest of the minority culture.

The Harlem Renaissance

Self-transformation came in the form of the Harlem Renaissance, but calling the Harlem Renaissance a renaissance, or rebirth, is an error, a misnomer, because the creativity of the African American community, which blossomed during the period, had never had a birth. But Booker T. Washington and W. E. B. Du Bois were the forerunners of the cultural wave that became the Harlem Renaissance. The Silent Protest Parade on July 28, 1917, organized by the NAACP, was the "first nonviolent mass protest by blacks. It would set the stage for the civil rights movement three decades later" (Hill 26).

If one event can be said to have initiated the Harlem Renaissance, it would be the famous dinner at the Civic Club, "New York's only integrated upper-crust club," to which "all the Harlem literati were invited" by Charles Spurgeon Johnson to celebrate the 1924 publication of Jessie Fauset's first novel, *There Is Confusion*, but the event became "a full-scale celebration of African-American literature" (Hill 59). Johnson was a sociologist whose work centered on racism. He believed that "people would need to see the souls of African Americans in order to understand them, and that that could only be done through the arts" (57). White editor Paul Kellogg spoke with some of the writers after the dinner and "offered Charles S. Johnson control of the March 1925 issue [of *Survey Graphic*] which would be devoted entirely to black culture . . . . Johnson quickly enlisted critic and essayist Alain Locke as the editor of this special issue, which was titled

Harlem: Mecca of the New Negro. Nearly every writer of importance to the Harlem Renaissance was included" (63). *Survey Graphic* "billed itself as a monthly magazine for professionals who 'want to know of the living contributions of other professions where they overlap yours in the realm of common welfare'" (qtd. in Hill 62).

The repeal of Prohibition and the stock market crash of 1929 led to the demise of the Harlem Renaissance because "whites no longer had to travel uptown to drink alcohol" (Hill 128), and the depression caused layoffs of laborers. White patrons no longer had money with which to continue their support of African American arts. Hill writes, "Once opportunity disappeared, the artists of the renaissance began to divide more clearly into two camps. The younger artists believed the arts should celebrate blackness in all its variety and be truthful to life, whereas the older, more established ones felt the arts should function as propaganda to uplift the status of African Americans" (131). It was this lack of unity which allowed the Harlem Renaissance to fall apart.

The Negro "Problem" and American Democracy

Then in 1944, Gunnar Myrdal claimed that the way black people live represents a failure of Americans "to live up to their ideals" (270), that it contradicts American ideals, which are humane ideals. He writes that there is a social ethos and a political creed which, taken together, form what he calls the "American Creed," which has "high goals." Even though America is "conservative in fundamental principles," he writes, "*the principles conserved are liberal*" (274). (Emphasis in original.) Looking back at history, Myrdal states that "America got this dynamic Creed much as a political convenience and a device of strategy during the long struggle with the English Crown, the London Parliament and the various British powerholders in the colonies" (274). He goes on to state that the "American Creed is a humanistic liberalism developing out of the epoch of Enlightenment when America received its national consciousness and its political structure" (274). Another ideological root of the American Creed was

"Christianity, particularly as it took the form in the colonies of various lower class Protestant sects, split off from the Anglican Church" (275), and a third was "English law" (277). But Americans have failed to live up to their ideals, Myrdal claims, shown in "the status accorded the Negro in America [which] represents nothing more and nothing less than a century-long lag of public morals" (277). That the "Negro in America has not yet been given the elemental civil and political rights of formal democracy, including a fair opportunity to earn his living" is an "anachronism," which "constitutes the contemporary 'problem' both to Negroes and to whites" (278).

Richard Wright

Four years earlier, an African American author, Richard Wright, had vividly portrayed this "lag of public morals" and the lack of "the elemental civil and political rights of formal democracy" in a novel, his 1940 *Native Son.* Wright brings together in the jail cell scene (325-50) all the conflicting forces of society to speak their pieces about Bigger Thomas's life and how it has been shaped by these forces. Wright has told the reader about each of them separately, but in this scene he shows them to us all at once.

Bigger's mother, sister, and brother represent his ties to family; he seems to realize suddenly, in the cell, that he does have a family. His mother, of course, is willing to do anything, even work for the Daltons forever, to have Bigger's life spared. Vera is ashamed, but Buddy wants to help Bigger in some belligerent way, by killing. The larger community of Negroes is represented by his friends, Gus, Jack, and G. H. The minister represents the "turn the other cheek" philosophy of pacifists like Booker T. Washington. Mr. Dalton does indeed, just as the introduction tells the reader (xxl), represent capitalism. The capitalism he represents tends to throw money at problems, hoping they will go away. For instance, he gives millions of dollars to blacks, and buys ping-pong tables for their young people, but he refuses to rent a house to a Negro family unless it is in a certain part of town. He claims not to have caused any suffering and disclaims responsibility for the state of the world. Mrs. Dalton, even blind, has done perhaps more good than any of the other whites represented here: she has seen her previous chauffeur through night school and helped him to a better existence.

Mary is not in the scene, of course, but her attempts to help the Negroes deserve mention here: they were sincere, but naive and misguided. Jan and Max, the communists, are here to argue against the capitalism that Mr. Dalton represents and to argue for a social change for the Negro race; they seem to be more informed than the other whites about the cultural situation. As a defense lawyer, Max also stands in opposition to the prosecutor. The State's Attorney, Buckley, is shown to be a politician, more concerned with reelection and getting to his club than with justice. He knows all of the tricks about how to elicit confession. He also represents the injustice of the justice system. Even though journalism is represented in this scene only in the form of the newspaper Bigger has just finished reading, Wright sees journalism as a force in society that fans the flames of hatred between the races.

Because Wright did not break with communism until 1942, according to the "Chronology" (557), it seems that he is touting communism in this novel as a means to social justice for Negroes. Therefore, his vision would seem to lie with Max in this novel. But from the present perspective, knowing that Wright did indeed break with communism a mere two years after the publication of *Native Son,* the reader may wonder what Wright's next choice of cures would be for the social ills of this country–how he would have written this novel in 1942.

Since Myrdal and Wright wrote, however, civil rights legislation has been passed and schools have been desegregated. Since then, an African American woman, Toni Morrison, has received the Nobel Prize for Literature and an African American man, Barack Obama, has been elected President of the United States.

Latinos

When the colonized Mexicans gained independence from Spain in 1821, Spain had governed Mexico for 300 years. A mere 25 years later, the fledgling nation found itself involved in a war against the United States, which by that time, 1846, had become a respected nation, having defeated the British twice.

After two years of war, the Americans went home with enough land to produce five new states and parts of two others. Some of the Spanish-speaking Mexican families who inhabited that territory had been there for the entire 300 years and some, from their American Indian heritage, had been there since before written history. Suddenly, overnight, they found themselves citizens of a foreign land which spoke a foreign tongue. And to the rest of the Americans, these Spanish-speaking people were foreigners themselves, as they did not relinquish their culture when the boundary between the two countries moved. This was the beginning of the "two Mexicos" that Américo Paredes discusses in "The Folk Base of Chicano Literature." He writes that one of the Mexicos is "found within the boundaries of the Mexican Republic. The second Mexico—the '*México de Afuera*,' (Mexico abroad) as Mexicans call it—is composed of all the persons of Mexican origin in the United States" (6).

Other Mexicans crossed the border for work and then went back to Mexico as the seasonal work ran out. Paredes points out that they were competing with "former slaves" for work, and that their situation was "little superior" to that of the former slaves (11). But large numbers of immigrants from Mexico did not start to arrive in the United States until the Mexican Revolution of 1911. Paredes writes that these people were "another kind of Mexican immigrant," "political exiles" and "intellectuals" who were running away from the "fratricidal wars" (11) who "fled Mexico during the famous upheaval of 1910. Most arrived in the United States after the fighting had died down, in the period after 1915," writes Ramón E. Ruiz (xii). Mexican culture in "Mexico abroad" expanded and has been increasing, but changing, ever since.

Assimilationism

As Ruiz explains in "On the Meaning of Pocho," the *pocho* is the American child of Mexican parents, and his story "embodies the traditional ambivalence: the desire for acceptance by the 'Anglos' and the struggle for integration as a group and assimilation as an individual by the majority in American society and, conversely, the latent urge to win respect and recognition while maintaining a cultural identity" (x). The occasion for Ruiz's writing is to introduce the novel *Pocho*, written by José Antonio Villarreal and published in 1959. Ruiz writes that Villarreal's protagonist, Richard, has no "identity to replace that sense of inferiority that settled down upon" him (xii). Ruiz states that during the "'assimilationist' phase that prevailed then [at the time of Villarreal's writing], most Mexican Americans had rebelled against traditional values in their urge to join the American mainstream, that, is, when occasionally they had lifted their sights beyond the local community" (viii), indicating a relationship to both the majority and the minority cultures. Self-transformation can be seen, however, when, after the time of the novel's writing, the Chicano movement was initiated, with its "ideological bonds" which united "young militants" (xii). Whereas Villarreal "carefully draws distinction between 'Mexicans' and the 'Spanish' population," the Chicano movement proclaims a "unity of all Spanish surname people" and believes in the "existence of common bonds between Mexican-born Americans, Mexican-Americans, the hispanos [sic] of New Mexico who trace their ancestry back to Spanish colonial days, and even the descendants of the Californianos" (xii). To Villarreal, the "'Spanish' formed another population bloc," one which derives from "the early settlers of California when Spain controlled the Golden State" (xii).

The Chicano

The concepts of "the borderlands" and "border crossing" have become widely accepted recently because cultural critics have given new meaning to them. The idea of the borderlands is useful in the study of Chicano/a literature and culture, but it means much more than "simply the geographic line that separates Mexico from the United States" (Gonzalez 280). According to Marcial Gonzalez, "it also refers to cultural, personal, linguistic, sexual, psychological, and perhaps even spiritual space" (282), and he emphasizes its importance to Chicano culture. Therefore, it is an idea that can be useful in an interpretation of Chicano/a literature and culture.

In "the first published collection of short stories dealing entirely with Mexican-Americans," his 1971 anthology, *The Chicano: From Caricature to Self-Portrait*, Edward Simmen has collected stories about Mexican Americans, many of them written by Anglos, published from 1869 through 1970. The point he makes from both the title of the collection and the divisions of the book is that Mexican Americans had been caricatured in early literature, but were portrayed more realistically during the 1930s and 1940s, and finally have been able to portray themselves in works of literature. These steps go hand in hand with the change in tone and attitude that Louis Owens describes in Native American literature. The caricature would produce outrage, which would move toward alienation and despair at being portrayed "realistically" by others, but finally, the writers could find their own identity and portray themselves.

In his preface, Simmen explains two possible origins of the term *Chicano* and briefly gives a history of its possible connotations. One possibility, he writes, is that the word is of Nahuatl origin, perhaps a derivative of the way the Indians pronounced *Mexicano*, dropping the first syllable. At one time, it was "merely a term of ethnic identification," but came later to be used as an insult from one Mexican American to another, an insult meaning "lower" class (xii). The other possible origin of the word that Simmen presents is that the suffix *-ano* was joined to the word for boy, *chico,* in the way it was joined to Mexico to make *Mexicano*.

It may therefore be "related to *chicazo*, meaning a poorly educated young man who aimlessly, as a vagabond, roams the streets" (xii), another derogatory use. Simmen's use of the term, however, coincides with what he calls "that 'new' American—the outspoken and active young Mexican-American who has *always* sought to identify himself with *La Causa* or 'The Movement'" (xiii).

In the introduction, Simmen states that the Mexican American is tired of being "exploited by management, ignored by labor, and quickly forgotten by 'promising' politicians" and is now "standing up and demanding—demanding attention, recognition" (15). He writes that the Mexican American is "following the blacks" in "making himself heard" and in "making his presence felt" (15). As universities have responded by offering courses that "examine his oftentimes forgotten cultural heritage as well as his dubious role in the 'alien' Anglo society" (15), opportunities for him to receive a liberal education have increased (26). Simmen states that, in the past, "no Mexican-American has been equipped or inclined to contribute to American literature" but that when Simmen writes in 1971, Mexican American writers have "the accuracy to make it [literature] realistic and interesting, the force to make it effective, and the subtlety and structural complexity to make it art" (26).

And Ruiz explains that the importance of Villarreal's novel is that it was published in 1959, by a writer who is "the first man of Mexican parents to produce a novel about the millions of Mexicans who left their fatherland to settle in the United States. Not until 1970 did another Mexican-American duplicate that feat" (vii). He calls this self-transformation "a pioneer attempt" and writes that the book has "immense historical value" because it reflects the opinions of Villarreal's day, which have "changed perceptively" by the time Ruiz writes in 1970 (vii). Ruiz calls Villarreal "a university-educated man of Mexican ancestry who interprets the struggle of his 'people' in the light of his day" (ix).

82

Richard Rodriguez

In 1993, in the introduction to his *Days of Obligation: An Argument with My Mexican Father*, Richard Rodriguez questions whether he is writing a book on competing theologies (xvi). His overt discussion of competing theologies, contained in Chapter Nine, "The Latin American Novel," indicates that that is at least one of the themes of the book.

Rodriguez seems to compare Catholicism, the passive, receptive, orthodox religion, to the active, emotional, liberal Protestantism; he calls himself Catholic and prefers the traditional and the orthodox. But Catholicism is not a religion indigenous to Latin America any more than is Protestantism. The story of the Virgin of Guadalupe (16-20) is the story of how Catholicism gained many Indian converts from their old religion ("a recruitment poster for the new religion"). But Rodriguez says that "Catholicism has become an Indian religion" and that "the locus of the Catholic Church . . . will be Latin America" by the end of the twentieth century (20).

He has already informed us that the Catholic priests, upon arrival in Mexico, sought out the Indians, whereas the Protestants in New England had not. The Protestants were more aloof, believing that "the central experience of faith was of the individual standing alone before God," whereas the Catholic experience is "the most communal of Christians" (176). He tells us that most of the Protestants in Latin America are evangelical Protestants, mostly Pentecostals, which he calls "emotional Christianity" and that central to their spirituality is "an unmediated experience of Jesus Christ" (176). The mediator which Protestants find unnecessary is, of course, the Catholic Church. Rodriguez says that Protestantism is a religion of the cities and believes that, since the population of Mexico has changed from seventy percent rural to seventy percent urban within the last fifty years, Protestants will soon outnumber Catholics in Latin America (177), which will be the population center of Catholicism (20), but Protestants will still be in the majority.

This conflict of religions is more than Catholic versus Protestant, however. It represents a conflict of cultures and of a worldview, a way of looking at oneself in relation to the rest of the world. It seems that Rodriguez prefers the old, orthodox ways because he has attained a measure of success under the old rules; indeed, he is considered exceptional. The new, liberal worldview would require that he develop some compassion for his fellow beings, would expect him to act, rather than be acted upon. In a more liberal view of the world, Richard Rodriguez may be one of those patriarchal "white elephants" that would be disposed of. He, of course, is smart enough to realize where he stands and defends his position rather than be toppled.

Asian Americans

In "Bamboo That Snaps Back!" Fred Ho likens the Asian Pacific American movement in the United States to bamboo, which "'snap[s] back' in a continuous history of resistance to oppression and struggle for full equality, dignity, and liberation" (240). Chinese American cultural activity has as a backdrop the Chinese laborers on the transcontinental railroad in the 1860s, and most of this cultural activity came from the Chinese opera. In the early twentieth century, the way Chinese immigrants related to the majority culture was marginalization: they were still confined by "both segregation laws and the threat of racist violence" and were unable to participate in other forms of American entertainment. The Japanese workers on the Hawaiian sugar plantations, who, unlike the Chinese, were allowed to bring their women, brought their folk songs with them, but also created a "unique Japanese (Asian) American working-class folk song form" based on their traditional songs but about their new experiences (246).

In the 1920s and 1930s, Asian Pacific American communities saw the "growth of Marxism and left-wing radicalism partially because of their own oppression, exclusion, and persecution, and partially in sympathy with the broadening struggle against colonialism and for national liberation in Asia. Like the Irish, Asian Americans related to the minority culture by bringing their own communities together in support of nationalism across the sea.

Many mainland Japanese Americans succeeded in agriculture, "often turning deserts into arable acreage," which was coveted by "greedy white racist agri-business" (Ho 246-47). They lost their land when the United States government seized more than 120,000 individuals and locked them up in "twelve desert detention camps" in 1942 (247). There they "created paintings, wrote poems and stories, made sculptures and gardens" (247); these activities are now known as "Camp Art" (247). Ho writes that, during the late 1960s and early 1970s, the "Asian movement emerged simultaneously on both coasts of the mainland . . . and in Hawaii" (251) in a sense of self-transformation.

Min Zhou and J. V. Gatewood discuss the restriction of Asian immigration to the United States beginning with the Chinese Exclusion Act of 1882, which was not repealed until 1943. World War II allies of the United States included all Asian countries except Japan, so the "yellow peril" started to become the "model minority." The 1965 Hart-Cellar Act "abolished the national origins quota system" (116) during a time of great unrest in the United States, the civil rights movement and protests against the war in Vietnam. The globalization of the United States' economy has influenced immigration policy, as well. According to Zhou and Gatewood, understanding the contemporary immigration situation "requires a reconceptualized framework that takes into account the effects of globalization, uneven political and economic developments in developing and developed countries, the social processes of international migration, and the role of the United States in world affairs" (119).

Multicultural Activism

The Asian American Movement, which began with the San Francisco State University strike in 1968, gave birth to the Red Guard party, which was strongly influenced by the Black Panthers. They were inspired by the Black Panther party's self-reliance and militant stance. Daryl J. Maeda writes that the Asian Americans "performed blackness" as they emulated the Black Panthers, which they saw as a model to resist assimilation into whiteness. Cross-identifications between African Americans and Asian Americans occurred, for example, when Japan was proclaimed the "'champion' of the 'dark and colored races'" by the Pacific Movement of the Eastern World in the 1930s, and "blacks flocked" to the movement, according to Ernest Allen, Jr. (qtd. in Maeda 94). Black Panthers used Chairman Mao's Red Book as part of their political education. Blacks admired Asian radicalism, but mostly across the Pacific, not in the United States (94).

The Asian American students at San Francisco State University who carried out a "counterhegemonic" (Umemoto 26) strike were joined by African American, Native American, Chicano, and Latino students. They struck for self-determination and the right to participate in democracy. Karen Umemoto writes that the strike represented the beginnings of a "New World Consciousness" (35). The Asian American revolution lasted from 1964 through 1969, but the 1968 strike was a major success in mobilizing minority groups to struggle against the hegemony.

Questions of Color, Questions of Identity

Ajantha Subramanian looks at Indians in North Carolina and writes that their culture should be understood not only "as an expression of an American immigrant . . . [but also as] a southern immigrant consciousness" (159). There is a high percentage of high-tech professionals in the Indian American community, for one reason because "The U. S. concern of global dominance in the arenas of science and technology precipitated a transnational wave of Western migration" (161). Other reasons are to gain economic self-sufficiency and alleviate poverty. Indian Americans are considered a "'model minority' whose public profile fits neatly into the logic of American multiculturalism" (162). Other reasons for this kind of identity are "the discrediting of racial ideology after World War II and the civil rights movement" (163). Even so, Indian Americans in North Carolina still suffer from racism. Subramanian suggests that their sense of community and their culture has served "Indian Americans, among others, as a means to claim white privilege and disown blackness" (164). Subramanian writes that "multiculturalism is a new hegemonic discourse" (176).

The black-white binary excludes other minorities, but "current race discourse oversimplifies the paradigm and fails to articulate the full cost" of abandoning it (Kim 332). Janine Young Kim discusses six dimensions of the black-white paradigm: descriptive, theoretical, political, historical, linguistic, and subversive. Kim looks at immigrants' rights and affirmative action through the paradigm and addresses the objection that the black-white paradigm is inapplicable to the Asian American civil rights agenda.

Min Zhou discusses how to define Asian Americans as white. She writes that few Americans of Asian ancestry are willing to identify themselves as Asian or Asian American, preferring to focus on the specific country of their origin. The "model minority" image from the mid-1960s has had at least two influences on Asian Americans. This kind of image influences Asian Americans to hold higher standards to distinguish themselves from average Americans. Accordingly, they "are judged by standards different from those applied to average Americans" (357). The image sets Asian Americans "apart not only from other minorities but also from whites" (357). Because most Asian Americans accept "white" as "mainstream, average, and normal," they tend to measure themselves and their descendants "materially" (358). Even though Asian Americans are now perceived in a more modern way, they still "have to constantly prove they are truly loyal American" (359). Zhou quotes Eric Liu on the concept of an Asian American as a "banana," meaning yellow on the outside, but white on the inside (354).

Even though many Americans claim multiracial backgrounds, it was not until 2000 that the American government allowed Americans to choose more than one race on their census forms. In their 2007 essay, "Intermarriage and Multiracial Identification," Jennifer Lee and Frank D. Bean discuss Asian Americans and their high rates of intermarriage with persons of another race. They state that intermarriage decreases the social distance between races and also decreases racial prejudice. They anticipate that "the multiracial population could rise to 21 percent by the year 2050" (384). They write that, while Latinos and Asian Americans see race as a "social and cultural construction rather than a biological category" (386), African Americans, perhaps as one result of the "one-drop" rule, are the "least likely to intermarry and the least likely to claim a multiracial identification" (389). They conclude that different groups show a difference in identifying themselves as multiracial, and the blending of races is not equally distributed across all ethnic groups.

These authors emphasize some features of contemporary Asian Americans, who encompassed "eleven national-origin or ethnic groups with populations exceeding 150,000" at the end of 1970 (Zhou and Gatewood 121). Both immigrants and their American-born children experience "being in America but not fully a part of it" (124). In order to avoid discrimination, Asian immigrants retreat to their own ethnic communities. Native-born Asian Americans live in a hybrid culture, with one foot in the culture of the United States, and one foot in the culture of their ancestors (128).

Maxine Hong Kingston

Asian American women, who are othered in the dominant community as minorities and marginalized and oppressed in their own community through gendered discourses of sexuality, can resist and reconstruct their identities for empowerment through a poetics of resistance. One Asian American woman writer in particular, Maxine Hong Kingston, especially in her fictionalized autobiography, *The Woman Warrior*, demonstrates how she both resists marginalization and reconstructs her own identity, in terms of both race and gender. She is one of the writers who was taken to task by members of her own ethnic group for what they said was selling out her own cultural heritage in favor of succeeding in the dominant society.

In her 2004 publication, *The Fifth Book of Peace*, Kingston uses her own position of activism as a young woman to critique women's responses to war and to show how women can, through those responses, build connections with men for mutual empowerment. The distinctly womanly responses to war indicate Kingston's reconstruction of women's power in our American society. Her book titles, naming both war and peace, are an interesting contrast. Especially in these last few years of our own country's waging of war in Afghanistan and Iraq, questions regarding women as warriors and women as peacemakers become relevant to these current international events.

Women warriors must struggle to overcome past injustices and empower themselves. The Woman Warrior, Maxine Hong Kingston herself, uses the pen as her sword, as she avenges injustices that are figuratively carved into her flesh. But words can do more than struggle against unfair gender roles and racism. They can be used to heal as well. *The Woman Warrior* brings two cultures together with words. *The Fifth Book of Peace* performs the necessary healing rites for self-transformation for war veterans, again with words. According to one critic, "Kingston seems to place her heroine's power in the ability to see humanity as a unity" (Chua 149).

To find a strong female role model, the protagonist Maxine in *The Woman Warrior* looks into the ancient Chinese culture to find the legend of Fa Mu Lan. As Maxine transforms herself into the woman warrior, she becomes strong enough to bridge the cultures and locate her own self-confidence. In her version of the legend, Maxine becomes the woman warrior by merging both soldier and student writer. Fa Mu Lan must subvert gender roles; she does this by disguising herself as a man. But this is dangerous business, she says, because the "Chinese executed women who disguised themselves as soldiers or students, no matter how bravely they fought or how high they scored on the examinations" (*The Woman Warrior* 39). This leader feeds her army and sings to them. She says, "My army did not rape, only taking food where there was abundance. We brought order wherever we went" (17).

Kingston also uses the legend of Ts'ai Yen, the captured poetess who fought alongside her barbarian captors. The traditional Chinese version of the legend emphasizes her return to her own people, but Kingston's version emphasizes the music she brings back from the "savage lands" (209), pairing her with the woman warrior who sings to her army. This singing also indicates that something beautiful, something soothing, can come from a negative experience. Transformation can take place.

There have always been concerns about women in combat in both the Western and the Chinese traditions. In his *Republic*, Plato considered the idea and decided that women should be allowed to serve as Guardians. More recently, James R. Aubrey discusses the class in which he taught *The Woman Warrior* at the United States Air Force Academy in 1985. This classroom was made up of mostly "prospective [male] warriors" (82), along with a few female cadets, who were not considered warriors, not allowed to participate in combat, and so were allowed entry not "on the basis of merit" nor "in proportion to their numbers in the American population," as were minority groups. These women are not disguised: they stand out through "such visual markers as hair style, body shape and size, and clothing (women's uniforms are not exactly uniform with the men's uniforms)," Aubrey writes (83).

Acknowledging that military traditions privilege masculinity, Aubrey sees some of Kingston's chapters as "text about the transformation of art" (84), including creative writing. Kingston imagines a "verbal discourse that transcends the conventions of gender" (84-85). Aubrey sees that "any kind of creative art has become not just an index of sanity, but a means to transcend cultural difference" (85). He says, "*The Woman Warrior* celebrates not military heroism but instead, metaphorically, the self as artist and the artist as social reformer" (85).

Many contemporary novels stress the relationship of humans to the rest of the world (other humans, nonhuman animals, the cosmos) as a spiritual relationship. In several of these works, the authors emphasize the healing power of love, the power of the individual, and the power of the word.

In Kingston's *Tripmaster Monkey: His Fake Book*, a later novel, eastern religions are referred to constantly, usually overtly, but sometimes more subtly. But the whole novel is an account of syncretism, of assimilation, and Chinese religions, legends, and traditions balance the American "religion" of literature. At least one critic claims that Kingston's reasons for writing this book include showing the male Chinese American writers who ignored her first two books that she, too, could be part of the tradition.[4] She draws on Taoism, Confucianism, and Buddhism, as well as the *Tripitaka*, to demonstrate her intimacy with Asian culture; she mentions an American writer or text on almost every page to demonstrate her intimacy with American culture. From this point of view, Kingston herself becomes the Woman Warrior of her first book. The protagonist of *Tripmaster Monkey*, Wittman Ah Sing (as in Walt Whitman's "I Sing America"), represents the melding of the two cultures in Walt Whitman's Transcendentalism, which combined eastern mysticism with the Quaker inner light.

Tibetan scholar Chögyam Trungpa, in *Shambhala: The Sacred Path of the Warrior*, describes a warrior as one who has a tender heart and who has experienced fear. He writes, "In order to experience fearlessness, it is necessary to experience fear. Acknowledging fear is not a cause for depression or discouragement. Because we possess such fear, we also are potentially entitled to experience fearlessness. True fearlessness is not the reduction of fear, but going beyond fear." He continues that "discovering fearlessness comes from working with the softness of the human heart" (47).

---

[4] Not all male Chinese American writers ignored her writing. Frank Chin published "This Is Not an Autobiography!" in 1985, referring to Kingston's first work, calling it a "fake book." Her response appears in the subtitle of her next work, *Tripmaster Monkey: His Fake Book.*

The softness of the human heart can bring about the discovery of fearlessness. In the ideal, "warriorship is that the warrior should be sad and tender, and because of that, the warrior can be very brave as well. Without that heartfelt sadness, bravery is brittle, like a china cup. If you drop it, it will break or chip. But the bravery of a warrior is like a lacquer cup, which has a wooden base covered with layers of lacquer. If the cup drops, it will bounce rather than break. It is soft and hard at the same time" (Trungpa 50), very much like Fa Mu Lan's army in Kingston's story.

Kingston may have herself had opportunity to experience this sadness and tenderness of heart which leads to bravery and warriorship. In September 1991, while returning from her father's funeral, Kingston discovered that the wild fires in California had destroyed her home, along with the manuscript of *The Fourth Book of Peace*, which she envisioned as a contemporary continuation of the legendary Chinese Three Lost Books of Peace. Nothing remained of the novel except "a black block of pages," she writes (34). As a consequence of these disasters, Kingston wrote her next work, *The Fifth Book of Peace*, which retells the novel in progress, details her trip to find her home among the burned-out ruins of her neighborhood, and reiterates her "call to veterans of all wars to help her convey a literature of peace" through their and her writings (239). This section describes in detail the anguish that these soldier-writers deal with as they pour their experiences of war and remembrances onto paper and heal themselves, and thus the world.

The Irish in America

Americans still harbor prejudices against the Irish Catholic identity, even as Irish Americans have attempted to transform themselves from immigrants to an ethnic community. Early immigrants from Ireland came to the United States not only for opportunity but also because conditions in Ireland did not allow the sustenance of so many people. Famine conditions were not the only reason they left their homeland; there was also the matter of families' dividing their little bit of land among their sons. Since the majority of the Irish were Catholics who traditionally have large families, they were literally running out of land; the small amounts they were able to divide among their many sons could not support a family. Later, the G. I. Bill "accelerated" Irish immigration during the postwar period, and their service in the United States military contributed to the evolution of the Irish American identity. According to Linda Dowling Almeida, in Ireland in the 1960s and 1970s, new government programs led to an increase in "marriage and fertility rates" while educational opportunities . . . expanded, employment rose and net out-migration dropped" (554). At the same time, United States' immigration law "changed," eliminating "national origin as the basis for immigration" (554), and so immigration from Ireland tapered off. As the Irish immigrants attempted to create an American identity for themselves, the high point of the Irish pride in ethnic identity came with the election of John Fitzgerald Kennedy as United States President in 1960 (557).

Whereas early immigrants from Ireland knew that they would never be able to return home again, owing to the famine conditions in Ireland and the expense and hardships of travel across the Atlantic, later immigrants, by the end of the twentieth century, did not "consider their time in America to be a permanent situation as did most of their predecessors. Their experience in the United States was complicated by the fact that most entered as illegal aliens and never fully integrated themselves into the mainstream of American life" (Almeida 562). As well, the Irish communities had disappeared, owing to their aging population (562) and "affluence, suburban life, public education, intermarriage with spouses of different faiths and ethnicities" (556). Thus the Irish American identity has been weakened.

Margaret Lynch-Brennan follows the history of Irish immigrant women from domestic servants to householders in their own families. In the mid-1900s, immigrant Irish women found work in the United States as domestics, which had two important results: their jobs made them "acceptable to Americans and gave Irish women an opportunity to learn and internalize American middle-class values and social conduct, which they could in turn apply as a means of propelling their families up the social scale" (332). Although from the 1830s to the 1930s African Americans predominated in the service areas, requiring Irish women to compete with them for jobs, Irish women still "fit the bill for an employable servant in the United States" (334). By working in middle-class American homes, Irish domestics learned social mores which were applicable to their own families, allowing them more rapid assimilation into the mainstream culture.

Irish Nationalism in the United States

Both Daniel Patrick Moynihan and Kevin Kenny agree that Irish nationalist sentiments have contributed greatly to the Irish identity in the United States. Kenny calls attention to the independence movement of the early twentieth century; he writes, "constitutionalist nationalists on both sides of the Atlantic reorganized themselves at the turn of the century" (293). World War I became a turning point as the "hard-line Irish republicans" decided to launch a rebellion at that time. Even though the Easter Rising of 1916 failed, the insurrection advanced Irish nationalism to the status of "a mass movement for the first time since the 1880s" (Kenny 295). But the eventual "establishment of the Irish Free State and later the Republic of Eire . . . has substantially put an end to the agitation for Irish independence which contributed so much to the maintenance of the Irish identity in America" (Moynihan 498). Moynihan writes that the ethnic identity of the Irish is fading because of "the decline of immigration, the fading of Irish nationalism, and the relative absence of Irish cultural influence from abroad on the majority of American Irish" (497). Moynihan points out that the large numbers of Catholic Irish who participated in what the Irish called "The Great Hunger" emigration of 1846-1850 were kept out of the political life of the country for a century by other Americans. When they did become part of the political life of the country, a sizeable part of their community became Irish Catholic Democrats, which caused New York to become "the first great city in history to be ruled by men of the people, not as an isolated phenomenon . . . , but as a persisting, established pattern" (Moynihan 479).

Irish American Writers

Daniel J. Casey and Robert E. Rhodes note a tradition among Irish American writers. They indicate that a "hyphenate literature" is all about a search for identity which "plays itself out in a perhaps never-ending, complicated process of both assimilation and affirmation" (649). As the "Famine immigrants" arrived in the United States in the mid-nineteenth century, they were stereotyped in ways that caused them "to disavow the past and emulate the Yankee work ethic" (650). By the time a hundred years had passed and an Irish American, Eugene O'Neill, had won the Nobel Prize for Literature (the first Nobel Prize awarded to a playwright), the United States had seen literary contributions from Frank McCourt, Betty Smith, F. Scott Fitzgerald, and many other Irish writers. O'Neill's work "magnifie[d] Irish-American dysfunction and failure" (652), while Fitzgerald's novels moved progressively from a "rejection of the Irish, to a moderate acceptance of them, to an Irish-American hero's victimization by wealth and power" (653). Betty Smith's work presents the "sense of desperation" felt by so many poor Irish Americans and "captures the ambience of cold-water flats with empty larders and Tammany-sponsored children's excursions up the Hudson River" (652). Many of these writers were, like Fitzgerald, afflicted "by this intense social self-consciousness" (Fitzgerald qtd. in Casey and Rhodes 653). But by the middle of the twentieth century, there "was no longer a preoccupation with covering their 'scars of immigration'" (654) and they had collectively produced a "hybrid" Irish character. As the Irish immigrants, most "now third- and fourth-generation Americans" (655), gained access to the universities, they learned "literary traditions that deny old American and British stereotypes" and now "explore American themes and give voice to the American imagination" (661), as Bret Harte had recommended in 1899. The postwar period saw the appearance of regional differences among the Irish American writers. One of these regional writers was Flannery O'Connor, whose work "expressed an intellectualized Catholicism rather than an Irish consciousness" (657).

Flannery O'Connor

It is very difficult, if not impossible, to understand Flannery O'Connor's stories without thinking of her own situation in life, struggling with a debilitating illness which caused her death at the young age of 39. Her stories "often depict ...human alienation [and] are concerned with the relationship between the individual and God" ("O'Connor," Merriam-Webster 824). She writes about "the struggle of souls to know themselves, to escape evil, and to reach God" (Hart 483), similar to the struggle for self-transformation in the face of the majority culture. In her stories, "[o]ften the adult child is, like O'Connor, forced to return from the city due to illness and to leave behind an exciting life of the mind discovered there, one that is missing from the solitary existence of rural life" (Margaret Anne O'Connor 642). According to Nina Baym and her co-editors, O'Connor's stories are full of "hair-raising jokes that centrally inform her writing," and the author refused "to indulge in self-pity over her fate" (2094). It is easy to find parallels to O'Connor's own life in two of her stories, "The Life You Save May Be Your Own" and "Good Country People."

As a matter of fact, the two stories are actually the same story with different settings and circumstances. In both stories, an adult daughter lives alone with a mother in an isolated area; in both stories, a strange man outwits them both and takes something valuable away from them. In each case, the valuable thing that is stolen is their spirit, their soul—which, in each case, suffers from neglect and disuse.

In "The Life You Save May Be Your Own," the spirit is represented by the car which has been garaged for fifteen years: "'That car ain't run in fifteen year,' the old woman said. 'The day my husband died, it quit running'" (2122). The spirit, or soul, is associated with the masculine, while the body, represented by the house and land, is associated with the feminine. Mr. Shiftlet says, "'The body, lady, is like a house: it don't go anywhere; but the spirit, lady, is like a automobile: always on the move . . .'" (2127). The house and land, along with the virginal body of the young Lucynell, are what the old lady has to offer the stranger. So offer she does, linking the idea of the deed to the property and the girl through "'the courthouse'" (2127) even though the stranger warns her that "'nowadays, people'll do anything anyways'" (2123) and says, "'don't ever let any man take her away from you'" (2124).

The stranger can be a distorted Christ figure in this story: with his "half an arm," "his figure formed a crooked cross" (2122); in addition, he says he is "'a carpenter'" (2124); he is "'a moral intelligence!'" (2125). He plans to get the car, the masculine, the spirit, running again. He gets the car running again, he gets the girl, and he even gets some money from the old lady; but he's a grotesque Christ figure whose body is incomplete. He calls upon God, after he leaves the girl and his next intended victim jumps out of the car, to "'Break forth and wash the slime from this earth!'" (2129). His prayer is answered in the form of a storm that he "race[s] . . . into Mobile" (2129). He apparently stays just ahead of the wrath of God in all his dealings. The question that remains at the end of the story is not whether Shiftlet beats the storm, but What happens to the young Lucynell? Has she profited from this escapade?

In "Good Country People" O'Connor sets up the same situation with minor differences. Where the girl in the first story is innocent, the daughter in this story has been away and become educated and sophisticated. The spirit in this family is represented by the Bible that does not reside in the parlor as was the custom at the time. The mother lies that her daughter is an atheist and does not want the Bible on display, so the mother keeps it beside her bed. But the daughter may really be an atheist; to her it is the artificial leg that is sacred: "She took care of it as someone else would his soul, in private and almost with her own eyes turned away" (2141). Again, a strange man tricks the daughter into parting with something valuable and sacred, her artificial leg.

O'Connor is usually considered a Southern, or regional, writer, and her Irishness is seldom mentioned, possibly because she does explore "American themes and give voice to the American imagination" (Casey and Rhodes 661), harkening again back to Bret Harte's 1899 recommendation.

Women

Nancy Chodorow, a psychoanalyst, writes that "It becomes important to men to have a clear sense of gender difference, of what is masculine and what is feminine, and to maintain rigid boundaries between these" ("Gender" 484). She also suggests that gender is a learned behavior, that "gender difference is not absolute, abstract, or irreducible" (477). In "The Fantasy of the Perfect Mother," Chodorow and Susan Contratto conclude that the tendency to "blame the mother" also fits into cultural patterning. This cultural patterning oppresses women, and that oppression is what feminists want to change; we find protests against this kind of oppression in literature by American women no matter their ethnicity.

Even though the first feminist movement had succeeded in gaining suffrage for women, there were still activists who sought greater rights for women, along with peace and social justice. From 1946 until they were silenced by the House Un-American Activities Committee (HUAC) and the United States Department of Justice in 1950, the Congress of American Women worked toward those very goals (Swerdlow 296). At its beginning, as a branch of the Women's International Democratic Federation, the organization recruited many "women who believed that the attainment of genuine equality for women required the mobilization of 'the masses'" (299). It also recruited "a large number of African American women because of its strongly articulated, and frequently implemented, stand against racism" (299). Its leadership included women "of varied social, racial, and political backgrounds" (301). Because of politics, the "cold war repression of foreign policy dissent, and postwar sexual politics" (297), the organization collapsed and "effectively dissolved the conscious connection between feminism, social reform, and peace protest that was a political given for the postsuffrage peace activists" (312).

Women made great contributions during war time, but there was racial separation even then. Nikki L. Brown discusses the work of Alice Dunbar-Nelson in critiquing the racial caste system, which calls for a reexamination of possibilities of social reform during war time. Mary Helen Washington writes that we still "have no sense of the important cultural and political work done by United States blacks in the Cold War decades" (183) and points out literary works by Alice Childress, Lorraine Hansberry, and Claudia Jones as examples.

Joyce Antler explains the Emma Lazarus Federation of Jewish Women's Clubs, which "illuminates a model of . . . 'linked' identity, combining elements of gender, culture, politics, race, and ethnicity in a flexible, yet unusually engaged, fashion" (270). The organization was initially a division of the Jewish People's Fraternal Order of the International Workers Order, a labor union formed in the early twentieth century. The Emma Lazarus division was organized by three women with similar working-class backgrounds "to combat anti-Semitism and racism, provide relief to wartime victims, and nurture positive Jewish identification through a broad program of Jewish education and women's rights" (273). When the division became an independent organization, its focus changed to emphasize "the progressive voice of labor as the hallmark of democracy and called for coexistence with the Soviet Union" (274). As well, its program emphasized that "knowledge of Jewish tradition should extend beyond holidays and artifacts to an understanding of vital Jewish contributions to American history and democracy" and sought to "promulgate the neglected history of American Jewish women" (275). The Emma Lazarus Federation saw its primary duty as developing "curricula on such subjects as the contributions of dissident women from Anne Hutchinson to Ethel Rosenberg and the role of America's working women in the Lowell [Massachusetts] mills and garment sweatshops" (279). It has made a tremendous contribution to the women's rights and abolition movements and campaigned for human rights. Its lasting goals are "the elimination of anti-Semitism and racism, the campaign for women's rights, support for the state of Israel, and world peace and consumers' issues" (280). Instead of seeing the women of the federation as having a homogeneous identity, they should be considered "as women, as Jews, as proud members of the working class, as radical activists, and as Americans sensitive to the horrors of race prejudice," writes Antler (294).

Literary criticism of American women's writing has several features. Many critics pay attention to the feminism of literary history. For example, Nina Baym's *Feminism and American Literary History* insists on putting women into the history of American letters. Feminists focus on the link between women's writings and other social aspects, such as the problems of children, the gender gap, and women's political issues. A number of essays in Linda K. Kerber's *U. S. History as Women's History: New Feminist Essays* refer to these problems. Frequently critics emphasize the racial and cultural contexts of women's writing. Cheryl A. Wall's *Worrying the Line: Black Women Writers, Lineage, and Literary Tradition* and Carol S. Manning's *The Female Tradition in Southern Literature* are just two examples. Karen E. Beardslee, in her *Literary Legacies, Folklore Foundations: Selfhood and Cultural Tradition in Nineteenth- and Twentieth-Century American Literature*, notes that women's "piecing" traditions can be found in literary works and suggests that women's cultural traditions and folklore can be an approach to literary criticism of women's writing.

Southern Women Writers

Because of the de-valuing of women's writing, the Southern Renascence has been believed to have started with the Fugitives and the Agrarians in Nashville. But Carol S. Manning suggests that the real Southern Renascence began "in the midst of the turn-of-the-century women's movement with the voices and writings of scattered women" (52). She writes that there has been "a neglected feminist vein in Southern literature" (52). Anna Shannon Elfenbein offers evidence that Southern women authors of the 1930s "occupy an important place in the Southern female tradition of literary protest against oppressive man-made codes" (194). In *Twentieth Century Southern Literature*, J. A. Bryant, Jr. states that "Fiction in the South was already on its way to becoming largely a woman's province" by the 1940s (147). Flannery O'Connor, a Southern woman writer as well as an Irish American writer, is one example of American women writers, from many cultural backgrounds, who also protest the cultural bias against females. Another is Diana Abu-Jaber.

Diana Abu-Jaber

In this era of globalization with its transnational cultural flow, the role of identity construction in the West and throughout the world remains problematic. Some transnational women have never been to their home country but still must construct a national identity. As well, they must define their gender in cross-cultural spaces where ideas of identity take on special meaning. We can find such hybrid identities represented in American literature.

Women from the Middle East, for example, who construct a separate sexual identity from that of the idealized and essentialized notion of pure womanhood, struggle to depict their identities in troubled third world territories and, given resurgent debates on nationalism in the West over the past few years, it has become difficult for them to negotiate identity even in first world spaces like the United States, where such individualism is encouraged. Contemporary literature offers critical insights on issues such as identity politics and representation.

Diana Abu-Jaber wrote her first two novels, about the Arab American community, ten years apart: *Arabian Jazz* and *Crescent*. One is set in small-town New York and one in urban California. The protagonists of the novels are young unmarried women, both of whom have lost their mothers, who would have been a role model for them. But even absent mothers have a great influence on the families that they have left behind. The young women must attempt to find out for themselves how to be a woman in the United States, even though they each have strong ties to an Arab culture and each is raised by an Arab man.

As well, the new generation of half-Arab, half-American children must grow up and manufacture their own space from which to make their voices heard much the same as the Native American, African American, Latina, and Asian American women writers have, as I have pointed out elsewhere (*The Voice of the Oppressed in the Language of the Oppressor*). A look into absences in her novels reveals that Diana Abu-Jaber has made a space for Arab American literature in the multicultural atmosphere in which we now read American literature much as her protagonists, daughters of American mothers and first-generation immigrant fathers, must make a space for themselves and discover their own identities.

Immigration from the Middle East to the United States began before World War I, according to Michael W. Suleiman in his book *Arabs in America*: "The early immigrants spoke Arabic and came from a predominantly Arabic culture and heritage, but they did not think of themselves as 'Arabs'" (12). These early immigrants were called by various names, such as "Asians, 'other Asians,' Turks from Asia, Caucasian, white, black, or 'colored'" (12), and their relationship to the majority culture was an eagerness to assimilate into the dominant American society. These Arab immigrants "strove to remove any differences, except perhaps food and music, that separated them from the general American population" (8-9). As well, they refrained from teaching their children their own native Arabic or teaching them about their Arab heritage (9). However, when their identity was questioned, early Arab Americans "developed a two-cultures thesis. . . ." (12). The thesis was that, ". . . although America was the most advanced country in the world in science, technology, and industrialization, the East was spiritually superior. . . . As the children grew up immersed in American society and culture while simultaneously exposed to a smattering of Arabic at home and some Arabic food and music, they often found themselves experiencing an identity crisis of some kind, mainly resulting in rootlessness, ambiguity, and a fractionalized personality" (12), especially the Arab women.

Later immigrants from the Middle East, however, attempted to keep themselves separate from American social customs by not imitating them and by not mixing with Americans either socially or through marriage (Suleiman 10). Whereas the early immigrants thought of themselves as "sojourners" who would return to their homelands, the later immigrants "were anxious to live full and productive lives" in the United States (10). According to Suleiman, present-day Arab Americans exhibit a "combination of the diversities of the early and more recent immigrants" (10). He goes on to say, "By 1967, members of the third generation of the early Arab immigrants had started to awaken to their own identity and to see that identity as Arab" (10). Abu-Jaber's protagonists are much like the children who have been taught neither Arabic nor the Islamic religion; they have, however, been exposed to the music and the food from their fathers' homelands, one Jordan, the other Iraq.

In *Arabian Jazz,* Jemorah, the protagonist, is 29, almost 30; this novel appeared ten years before *Crescent,* in which the protagonist is 39, going on 40. In *Arabian Jazz,* the protagonist has a sister and a Jordanian father; it is her Irish-American mother who has died and abandoned the family. Like the uncle in *Crescent,* the father tells instructional stories, but he also tells stories through his music. He uses drumming as a way to deal with the loss of his wife, who has died during a visit to Jordan. Matussem, the father, raises his daughters alone in the United States, with some assistance from his married sister, their aunt Fatima, who is determined to find suitable Arab husbands for the girls, even trying to pair them with their cousins. The mother's death seems to be the center of the lives of both father and daughters and has been an influence on Fatima. However, it is the absence of four of Fatima's sisters that she carries with her throughout her life.

Matussem's sister Fatima blames his wife Nora for dying of typhus in Jordan out of spite; she tells Melvina, "'Your mother dies on purpose because she hates Arabs!'" (85). When her friend Estrelia asks Fatima: "'How do you contract typhus out of spite?'" Fatima answers, "'She doesn't get the vaccine, these is how! Who get typhus anymore? And die in one night, boom? Nobody but for silly-silly tourists who don't get their shots and come to Jordan to show so superior they are!'" (66). This exchange shows the difficulty of merging two cultures: Fatima fears that Nora feels superior to her; therefore, Fatima takes Nora's death personally.

Nora's parents blame Matussem for taking her to Jordan, where she has contracted the disease and died, and refuse to see their granddaughters because "'It hurts too much,' his mother-in-law had said to Jem, 'to see so much of our daughter mixed up with the body of her murderer'" (85). Like Sirine in *Crescent*, Jemorah and her sister need their American mother to teach them how to be Americans. When Jemorah sometimes thinks of having children of her own, she knows "that this idea emerged from another, deeper desire: a dream of rebirth, the longing to move more fully into her own life" (11); a child may give Jemorah a stronger, more universal identity, that of mother.

Even though Jemorah's guilt sometimes makes her feel "that the disease should have carried her off with her mother" (79), her sister, Melvina, who at the age of two had witnessed her mother's final moments, blames herself for not being able to remember her mother. This first encounter with death sets Melvina on her life's mission to defeat death by becoming a nurse, but not just any nurse— Melvina becomes the most knowledgeable, energetic, organized, and hard-working nurse of all. As well, she accomplishes this at a much younger age than most nurses.

Fatima, too, has had knowledge of death from an early age; when she is a child, she is forced to accompany her mother to bury alive her unwanted infant sisters at least twice and perhaps more times than she can remember (118-19). Even though she has helped bury her mother's unwanted infant daughters in Jordan, Fatima still wants Jemorah and Melvina to marry nice Arab husbands. This desire on Fatima's part exemplifies a point that Suleiman makes: that "Arab-American women have had more problems than their male counterparts in defining an acceptable or comfortable identity. . . . Women who have come from the most traditional countries of the Arab world have experienced a greater restriction of their freedom in the United States" because their men cannot cope with the "nearly complete freedom accorded to women in American society" (Suleiman 14). Fatima, raised in Jordan, is not only complicit in her own oppression, but she also strives to include her nieces.

Matussem wonders about these "unaccounted-for children" that Fatima has helped murder and is "afraid of being swallowed up, too, like his relatives, back into that history. Everything depended upon the new country" (187). Matussem knows, "watching and overhearing his sisters at night, that it was a bitter thing to be a woman" (187), which no doubt is a factor in his decision to raise his daughters in the homeland of their mother.

Matussem seems most assimilated of all into the new country: he sees people in his everyday existence that remind him of the people in his childhood stories from Jordan. And if he "recognized them everywhere, this country couldn't be such a foreign place after all" (98). But he still "liked to tell his relatives, 'I don't care how many *Bonanza* you watch, nothing get your brain ready for real America!'" (89). He refers to organized Arab functions as "'Arab hoe-downs'," and says, "'Jordan, Syracuse . . . it all the same wherever'" (51). It is his music that helps him to accommodate two cultures, the Arabian jazz of the title.

During a visit to his homeland, he discovers that other cultural accommodations have been made as well. Matussem's older sister Rima tells him that Fatima had been forced to assist in their sisters' murders and that Fatima had kept this secret all of her life. However, after the death of their parents, she and the other sisters have been bold enough to defy village and family customs to put up a tombstone for their murdered infant sisters, "engraved with the names of four girls, dating forty-two to forty-seven years past" (353). Rima tells him, "'We laid the babies to rest,' she said. 'You must tell Fatima. It's over. There's no one left to protect, nothing to do now but to mourn and reflect. We want her to come back, to visit and see her home and family again. To know that it's over'" (354).

Matussem is surprised to know that his sisters have also erected a stone for his wife:

> "But her grave is in America," he said, astonished.
>
> "I know. We had thought she might need a second bed," Rima said and smiled. "We thought her spirit might have become confused on such a long airplane ride back. So we had a second burial the week after you left. We wanted to give her soul ease." (354)

This act demonstrates that their gender is the connection that trumps their cultural differences.

As this novel closes, Jemorah has made a commitment to an American man. However, Jemorah is planning to return to school in California. But before she does, she has a symbolic wedding with her man in eating a wedding cake that Fatima has brought for a party: Ricky feeds the cake to Jemorah with his own fingers. They seal their commitments by dancing to the "jazz and trills of Arabic music" (374). *Arabian Jazz* uses the Arabic music that immigrant Arab parents had passed along to their American-born children to show some of the difficulties of discovering a hybrid identity that Arab women face in the contemporary world.

In *Crescent*, whose title is considered by many to symbolize Islam (Pearson), Abu-Jaber uses food to cross boundaries. In this novel, published ten years after *Arabian Jazz*, the unmarried female protagonist is 39, nearing her fortieth birthday. Sirine is cook for the lonely men of the Arab community in Los Angeles, students and professors, and works at a place where Arabic home cooking is served. Her Arab uncle has raised her after the deaths of her American mother and Iraqi father. The uncle tells an Arabic story about how to love, parts of which are interspersed throughout the story by the unnamed narrator of Sirine's life and loves. He tells her, "'If your parents were alive they would have showed you how to be in love. But you've only got your poor idiot uncle, so you've got to learn it all by yourself'" (83). Sirine has no American mother to teach her to be an American woman. When people tell Sirine she doesn't look half-Arab, "she feels like her skin is being peeled away. She thinks that she may have somehow inherited her mother on the outside and her father on the inside" (205), indicating her confusion regarding identity.

Sirine works for a Lebanese American woman, Um-Nadia, who owns the café where Sirine is the chef. Um-Nadia tells Sirine, "'They all come to me because we make something like a home in this country. . . . Men lose track of where they are. They miss their mother and father and sister. They don't know how to carry their homes inside themselves.' She looks closely at Sirine. 'You need to know how to do that'" (83). Sirine has had only a masculine viewpoint, however, in learning to grow into a woman.

Sirine makes a home for the lonely Arab students by cooking for them; at the same time she is haunted by her absent parents, whose occupation had kept them away from her much of the time in her childhood and who died when she was eight, abandoning her forever. To Sirine the smell of food cooking has always seemed to be a "magic spell" which could draw men to her because her father had always come to her mother's kitchen when he smelled food cooking. Hanif, the Iraqi professor who becomes Sirine's lover, longs for his home, but knows that he cannot go back at the risk of his life.

Nathan, an American student of Han, thinks of Han as being like an oryx. At one point, Han himself describes an oryx as "looking for his lost love, and they say he has to go away before he can find his way home again" (39). Her uncle tells Sirine that Han is "an exile–they're all messed up inside" and goes on to say that Han is an exile because he "can't go back. Because anything you can't have you want twice as much. Because he needs someone to show him how to live in this country and how to let go of the other" (47), just as Sirine has needed. She sees her own uncertainty regarding identity mirrored in her lover:

> What Han says [about his inability to return to Iraq] reminds her of a sense that she's had–about both knowing and not knowing something. She often has the feeling of missing something and not quite understanding what it is that she's missing. At the same

time, she's not sure what Han means about the dangers or why it was so difficult to leave–but she feels embarrassed to ask him and reveal her ignorance. She doesn't follow the news and now she feels ashamed that she's taken so little interest in her father's home country. (62)

"No one ever wants to cook for" Sirine, but when Han plans an "all-American evening" for her, Sirine tells him, "'But I'm not really all-American'" (68). As Han cooks the American meal for Sirine, he "seems excited" and is "intrigued by the new kind of cooking, a shift of ingredients like a move from native tongue into a foreign language" (68). As well, Han offers her a bit of his American meat loaf from his fingers: *"'Min eedi.* From my hand'," just as she remembers her father's feeding her in her childhood (71), like a sacrament. Sirine's answer to Han's meat loaf dinner is to prepare an "Arabic Thanksgiving" (192) dinner, at which the guests compare customs from Egypt and Lebanon (194) and sit around "'like a bunch of Americans with our crazy turkey'," according to Sirine's uncle (193).

Sirine is interested in finding out about her Arab identity through Han, who has recently arrived in the United States from his home in Iraq. Since Han teaches Islamic history and Arabic literature, he is able to inform Sirine about praying, which she thinks "sounds like singing" and makes her feel as she does when she is cooking: "'like when I stir a pot of soup, or when I knead the bread dough'," even though she has "never actually tried to pray before" (71). Sirine asks whether Han's religion, Islam, is the thing that defines him; but his answer is that he defines himself "'by an absence'" (161).

He believes in "'social constructions, notions of allegiance, cultural identity'" but the absence which defines his life is his exile. He says, "'Leaving my country was like–I don't know–like part of my body was torn away. I have phantom pains from the loss of that part–I'm haunted by myself. I don't know–does any of that make any sense? It's as if I'm trying to describe something that I'm not, that's no longer there'" (162). Sirine suggests, from her own experience

108

as an orphan, that missing his family is like death: "'you'll only be able to know them through your memory now'" (187).

After Han goes back to Iraq, Sirine notices in "her old Syrian cookbook" that the recipes are "little more than lists, no cooking instructions or temperatures, but scattered among the pages are brief reflections on the nature of animals, forest, flowers, people, and God. Sirine browses through the book, lingering equally over the reflections and the lists of ingredients, which seem to her to have the rhythms and balance of poetry" (315). The cookbook may be an analogy of the novel itself, a story about how Sirine learns to love, with brief Arabic stories among the pages of her story. At another time, Sirine's uncle tells her about stories–that they are "crescent moons; they glimmer in the night sky, but they are most exquisite in their incomplete state" (340), the absence of the middle.

In one of uncle's stories, this one about Omar Sharif, he identifies another absence: "'He became what they call *a star* in this country. In his right eye there were parties and girls, directors and scripts, money and fast cars. But in his left eye there was a sort of absence, a nothingness, that he couldn't quite identify. And if he tried to look straight at it, it would just float away in the maddening way that such things have'" (324).

In both of these novels, the female protagonist becomes allied with a man: Jemorah with an American, Sirine with an Iraqi. These alliances represent the coming together of two cultures. Abu-Jaber seems to recommend assimilation: In *Crescent*, as Sirine sits in on one of Han's classes, he contrasts Ernest Hemingway and Hafiz Mahfouz and asks, "'What does it mean to be an "Egyptian writer" or even a "Middle Eastern writer" anymore?' . . . 'The media is saturated with the imagery of the West. Is it even possible–or desirable–to have an identity apart from this?'" (98).

Lauren Sandler believes that it was once so, but perhaps no longer. She writes, "From the 1950s through the 1970s, Iraq's cities formed a first-world society within the third world. . . . In these urban areas, women had thrown off the black body-and-head covering *abbayas* and enrolled en masse in doctoral programs" (22). Today's woman in Iraq can only reminisce about those days, and the situation doubtless has undermined Iraqi women's sense of identity. Absences play a great part in this anxiety of identity formation. Diana Abu-Jaber treats the difficulties of women moving from the third world to the first; in her novels, she defines their difficulties by absences and their strength through Arabic music and food.

The Future of Feminism in America

The second feminist movement, of the late 1960s and 1970s, succeeded in raising the awareness of many Americans that women had not gained full citizenship. Even though the women activists in the 1970s pushed through an Equal Rights Amendment that had been first introduced in 1923, it was not ratified by enough states and so failed. Its failure "reflected a history of both female participation in politics and exclusion from power" (De Hart 217). Enthusiasm for women's rights soon led to several strong female political candidates for national office: Congresswoman Shirley Chisholm made a bid for the Presidency in 1972, and in 1984 Congresswoman Geraldine Ferraro was nominated by a major political party as its candidate for Vice President of the United States. In the twenty-first century, two women have made serious but unsuccessful bids for the backing of a major party in a Presidential election, Elizabeth Dole in 2000 and Hillary Clinton in 2008. In that same year, 2008, the male Republican candidate for President chose a female running mate.

Jane Sherron De Hart writes that the "defeat of the [Equal Rights] amendment demonstrated that political efforts by various subsets of feminist-oriented women representing different styles and strategies were a necessary, but not sufficient, condition for policy gains" (224). She foresees that "women will continue to employ the strategies and styles of political activism developed over the course of a century" (242). Her words have proved prophetic: in July 2009, the Equal Rights Amendment was reintroduced in the House of Representatives by Congresswoman Carolyn Maloney and Congresswoman Judy Biggert. The

Senate companion bill was to be reintroduced shortly thereafter. The sponsors hope to gain ratification by three more states, making a total of 38 ratifications, which is the required number for the amendment to become part of the United States Constitution. If the ERA is finally ratified, marginalized women will have not only figured in their own self-transformation but will also have changed again the notion of what it means to be American.

The Beats

Another group on the margins of American society in the 1940s, 1950s, and 1960s was a group of experimental writers and seekers who came to be known collectively as the "Beats," the "Beat poets," or the "Beat generation" and who were perhaps the most noticeable part of a larger artistic movement which also included Black Mountain College in North Carolina, known for its attempt to place the art experience, not the art profession, at the center of education. Perhaps the two most famous names from the group are Jack Kerouac, a French-Canadian immigrant studying at Columbia University, and Allen Ginsberg, a homosexual Jew from New York and a fellow student at Columbia. Others included William S. Burroughs, heir to the Burroughs office machine fortune, and Lawrence Ferlinghetti, who in 1955 opened the City Lights bookstore in San Francisco and who published the Pocket Poets series, including some of the Beats' work. These white males had grown up with the values of the dominant society, the recipients of all of the advantages of their privileged status. And, when they did grow up, they rejected those values as too stifling.

These men (and it was almost exclusively men), who had been born under the aegis of the dominant culture, were disgusted and dismayed at society's standards and flouted the dominant society's rules in several very important ways: through religion, drugs, sex, marriage, and crossing racial barriers. Because Kerouac thought he could show his readers what was happening in his mind as he wrote, he saw that traditional literary standards would be inadequate to his purpose. His discovery of Buddhism was important in this effort, and he attempted to use Buddhist concepts in his writing. At the end of the Beat era in the early 1960s, at least two important changes had come about in American society's values as a direct result of the efforts and the examples of these writers—a legal definition of obscenity in literature, and the emulation of the Beats' lifestyle by those imitators who moved from the "beatnik" phase into the hipster phase, or "hippie," who became the backbone of the 1960s counterculture.

The label *Beat* encompasses several traits of the movement; some of them are: beaten down, to be at the bottom looking up, the beat of the heart, and the beat of music, as the Beats were heavily influenced by jazz and frequently read their works to a jazz accompanist. But, especially for Kerouac, the term also includes the ideas of "beatific" and a spiritual quest for enlightenment or self-transformation.

In 1955, Kerouac and Ginsberg became acquainted with Gary Snyder and Philip Whalen, writers on the West Coast. It is important to note that Kerouac, Ginsberg, Ferlinghetti, Snyder, and Whalen all had a formal connection to Buddhism. For Kerouac, Ginsberg, and Snyder, the practice of sitting meditation is of primary importance to their creative work. Snyder himself became the hero of Kerouac's novel *The Dharma Bums*. Each of the Beats had a unique style, but they had a common mythical view of themselves. They all held a distrust of American politics and the American dream and saw a need for transnationalism as the dream, in their eyes, became a nightmare. They foregrounded the quest for self-discovery with an intense, restless enthusiasm and exhibited an interest in Surrealism in art, in which the image comes from the artist's unconscious. They considered conventional literary forms purposeless and therefore experimented with plot, syntax, diction, and meter. Kerouac's enthusiasm and experimental bent caused him to write *On the Road* on one long, continuous roll of paper so that he would not interrupt his spontaneity by changing paper in the typewriter. As a pioneer in a stylistic revolution, Kerouac was committed to the practice of spontaneous prose and aimed to "create an honest record of the writer's modes of perception" (Tonkinson 24). The Beat writers wanted to change not only themselves, but America itself.

One important change that did come about as a result of their writing is a legal definition of *obscenity*. Censorship of material considered obscene reflected the values of a conservative dominant society in the 1950s, the very values that the Beats disdained. Ginsberg's first public reading of his long and breathless "Howl" at San Francisco's Gallery Six caused an uproar leading to a police raid of City Lights and put Ginsberg's work on trial for obscenity; Ginsberg was acquitted. Then Burroughs had much difficulty getting his *Naked Lunch* published as a novel, so excerpts were published in a few journals. The first excerpt appeared in the last issue of the *Black Mountain Review*; the next was published in the *Chicago Review*, a journal sponsored by the University of Chicago. University officials were embarrassed when a newspaper columnist publicly denounced the excerpt as obscene, and they refused to allow publication of any further excerpts. Editor Irving Rosenthal and six staff members resigned and created a new journal, *Big Table*, in which they continued to publish chapters from *Naked Lunch* (Watson 281). When it was finally published in novel form, the city of Boston, Massachusetts brought obscenity charges against it in Massachusetts Superior Court (Watson 283). The case was appealed all the way up to the United States Supreme Court, where obscenity was defined by Justice William Brennan. His definition had three criteria for judging obscenity, and each criterion had to be met:

> 1. The dominant theme of the material taken as a whole appeals to a prurient interest in sex.
>
> 2. The material is patently offensive because it affronts contemporary community standards relating to the description or representation of sexual matters.
>
> 3. The material is utterly without redeeming social value. (qtd. in Watson 284)

Based on these criteria, *Naked Lunch* was judged not obscene by five of the seven justices, giving the American public a new freedom to read material that had heretofore been denied to them. In this way, the Beats changed American society.

Individually, the Beats were not marginalized. They were educated, white males, but they put themselves on the periphery of American society by rejecting the values of the dominant society as inauthentic. They used their dress, their drug use, and their interracial friendships to separate themselves from the white middle class, although most of them came from the middle class themselves. They felt a greater empathy instead with the marginalized minority groups.

According to Gary T. Mark in his 1967 article "The White Negro and The Negro White," a paradox existed between two special classes in American society. Mark demonstrates a dilemma between the Beats and the black bourgeoisie. The Beats rejected middle-class values and took their behavior models from lower-class Negroes, while the black bourgeoisie took a reverse attitude toward the Beats by accepting the values of the white bourgeois world.

Both classes faced the problem of social mobility, although the direction of their mobility was different. They both had difficulty being accepted by the whole society because "people who have been upwardly or downwardly mobile often have trouble being accepted" (Mark 171). Mark writes that the sexual behavior and the attitudes of Negroes and the Beats were different. Family stability and fidelity were taken more seriously by Negroes than by whites, while the Beats rejected the traditional middle-class attitude toward sex. It is not surprising, then, that homosexuality and extra-marital heterosexual sex are found frequently in works by the Beats.

Mark reveals that each of the two groups had a distorted image of the other, that their "behavior . . . [was] seen as exaggerated or inauthentic" (174). For example, the Negroes Kerouac liked were supposedly supersexed, narcotics-using, primitive, easy-going, spontaneous, irresponsible, and violent, according to Mark. The Negro characteristics which Kerouac reverences and wishes that he could share are stated in *On the Road* when "At lilac evening" Sal is walking through

> the Denver colored section, wishing I were a Negro, feeling that the best the white world had offered was not enough ecstasy for me, not enough life, joy, kicks, darkness, music, not enough night . . . I wished I were a Denver Mexican, or even a poor overworked Jap, anything but what I was so drearily, a "white man" disillusioned. All my life I'd had white ambitions (169-70).

But, Sal goes on, "I was only myself, Sal Paradise, sad, strolling in this violet dark, this unbearably sweet night, wishing I could exchange worlds with the happy, true-hearted, ecstatic Negroes of America" (170). This is where his white ambitions had brought him, and he finds himself outside of the dominant group.

Kerouac's Theory of Writing

Jack Kerouac's *On the Road* exemplifies Kerouac's theory of writing. In addition, the Buddhist ideas found in the novel reveal the prelude to Kerouac's attempt to instill Buddhist concepts into all of his subsequent writing. Kerouac's theory of writing and his *On the Road* characters reflect the Buddhist trikaya, or the concepts of body, speech, and mind; the structure of the novel both follows his theory and reflects the Buddhist practice of meditation.

Kerouac writes, in his "Belief & Technique for Modern Prose," that the writer should "sketch the flow that already exists in mind" and "see picture better" instead of thinking of words as he writes, because "something that you feel will find its own form." He further advises the writer: "Write for the world to read and see your exact pictures of it." In greatly simplified terms, it seems that Kerouac is advocating that the writer feel and see what is within himself and then attempt a spontaneous description of those feelings and sights so that the audience may also feel and see. As the mind eliminates, through meditation, "distinctions between matter and spirit, divinity and humanity, the sacred and the profane," the writer shares "these insights with others through . . . word" (Prothero 20). This kind of writing would be an experience in self-discovery for the writer, whose experiences could then be conveyed to the reader without the constraints of accepted literary form.

According to philosopher Stephen Prothero, the Beat writers were "wandering seekers of mystical visions and transcendence" (19), which they may have found in their meditations. As Allen Ginsberg writes in "Notes Written on Finally Recording 'Howl'," "Mind is shapely, Art is shapely. Meaning Mind practiced in spontaneity invents forms in its own image and gets to Last Thoughts" (28). Kerouac's spontaneous art, his Spontaneous Prose, springing from working with his mind, can be said to have its own, new form.

Discovery of self seems to be the basis for Kerouac's ideas about what writing is and how it should be done. From the very title of his "Essentials of Spontaneous Prose" it is obvious that Kerouac thinks that writing should be spontaneous. He goes on to exhort the would-be writer never to "after-think." Rather than later exerting control over the writing, Kerouac's "quest was for language—pure, natural, unadulterated language or the open heart unobstructed by what Kerouac saw as the lying of revision" (Weinreich 77).

Kerouac wants the "shaping" of experience to be more intuitive, less rational, distinct from earlier literary criteria. Kerouac's purpose in writing is to reflect mind spontaneously. In regard to pace and structure, Kerouac would cite what he calls the "Great Law of timing" and the "laws of Deep Form." On timing, Kerouac refers to the need to "speak now in own unalterable way"—in other words, to write spontaneously, without revision. This spontaneity will produce its own rhythm, or pacing, according to Kerouac.

An example of the rhythm that is found in breathless spontaneity can be seen in the last sentence-paragraph of Kerouac's novel *On the Road.* It must be read to be appreciated:

> So in America when the sun goes down and I sit on the old broken-
> down river pier watching the long, long skies over New Jersey and
> sense all that raw land that rolls in one unbelievable huge bulge

over to the West Coast, and all that road going, all the people dreaming in the immensity of it, and in Iowa I know by now the children must be crying in the land where they let the children cry, and tonight the stars'll be out, and don't you know that God is Pooh Bear? the evening star must be drooping and shedding her sparkler dims on the prairie, which is just before the coming of the complete night that blesses the earth, darkens the rivers, cups the peaks and folds the final shore in, and nobody, nobody knows what's going to happen to anybody besides the forlorn rags of growing old, I think of Dean Moriarty, I even think of Old Dean Moriarty the father we never found, I think of Dean Moriarty. (253-54)

The rhythm in this passage is certainly the one of flowing, uninterrupted thought that Kerouac asserts will come through his spontaneous writing method. And the description does give the reader a picture of what Sal sees when he remembers his association with Dean; in other words, his "exact picture" of the world. His enthusiasm for the spaciousness of the American landscape is found in several descriptive phrases: "the long, long skies"; "all that raw land"; "rolls in one unbelievable huge bulge"; "all that road going." The lack of traditional punctuation further contributes to the sense of breathlessness. As well, this passage reflects the blurring of boundaries that frequently occurs as a result of meditation.

As for structure, Kerouac specifically advocates following a fan-like form, which he likens to water running over a rock. Starting at the center of interest, the rock, the structure should flow in the outline of a fan until it trickles out completely. This plan follows the laws of Deep Form, he says. When one reads *On the Road*, it is evident that Kerouac uses the fan-like structure he espouses in "Essentials of Spontaneous Prose" to structure the whole book. He starts with the center of interest, Sal's involvement with Dean, at their first meeting. The narrative then flows over this rock with breathless excitement and fans out into separate adventures, consisting mostly of their search for identity in the face of a society of conformity and containment, until finally it trickles out with their separation and Sal's thinking of Dean on the pier at the end. Kerouac's Deep Form, the fan-like structure of water flowing over a rock, can be seen in this final paragraph as well. The water, the thought, flows over the rock, the pier, into a few spines that fan out: skies, star, God/ land, prairie, Iowa/ road, dreaming, complete night/ people, children, nobody/ anybody, Dean, Old Dean. Thus, it is apparent that, although Kerouac does not follow accepted forms, he does indeed use timing and structure in his writing.

Kerouac's *On the Road* characters further present his ideas. Sal and Dean consider the going more important than the getting there. When Kerouac says through Sal on page 104, "I had nothing to offer anybody but my own confusion" (a Buddhist term for lack of enlightenment), he is again asserting that these are his own experiences, spontaneously conveyed. Dean lives his whole life in bursts of breathless excitement: "he was simply a youth tremendously excited with life" (8). Regina Weinreich's own view of the Beat includes what she calls IT: "*On the Road* celebrates a new kind of hero, one who embodies IT, IT being a radiant moment when time stops and all is in the perpetual NOW. The hero who embodies IT lives in the present without thought to past or future" (77). This "radiant moment" represents the ecstasy which results from contact with the Dharmakaya. And Kerouac's description of Dean's and Sal's mad dashes across the continent and back again, their "romantic quest for the promise of America" (Weinreich 77), further illustrates the spontaneity of their lives.

Buddhist Concepts in Kerouac's Work

According to his literary executor, John Sampas, after Kerouac began studying Buddhism in earnest in 1954, he announced his intention to use a Buddhist outlook in all of his writing. He even wrote a life of the historical Buddha that would be understandable to the common person. Kerouac considered his early work to be "'Pre-enlightenment' work." Even though Steve Wilson writes, in his analysis of *On the Road* and *The Subterraneans*, that Kerouac has provided "the outlines of the path we are to follow" (315), Kerouac still thought of these works as "'Pre-enlightenment' work." In a 1955 letter to his literary agent, Sterling Lord, Kerouac wrote, "From now on all my writing is going to have a basis of Buddhist teaching, free of all worldly and literary motives so everything has actually worked out fine because in all consciousness I couldn't publish [*On the Road*] except as 'Pre-enlightenment' work" (qtd. in Sampas 12).

Kerouac must have had glimpses of the Absolute in his meditation practice, as the structure of the novel shows. George Dardess writes this about the structure of the novel: "The book begins with the narrator's construction of distinctions and boundaries; it ends with his discarding them . . . . The book moves from hierarchy to openness, from the limitation of possibilities to their expansion" (201). As a matter of fact, Dardess sees the final paragraph of the novel as one in which "temporal and spacial [sic] boundaries are obliterated" (201). This is the same paragraph which exemplifies what Kerouac called "The Essentials of Spontaneous Prose."

In the end, though, Dean cannot have an effective relationship with anyone; neither can Sal. Neither Kerouac nor Sal subscribes to Dean's idea of GOING; Sal is attracted to this idea, but he still feels the need for direction and serves as a foil to Dean. At the end of the novel, Sal becomes divorced from what Dean stands for; Sal cannot comprehend Dean any more.

Kerouac's life seems to have come to a similar end. According to Carole Tonkinson, Kerouac was "condemned as an enemy of the American way" (27). One later group, the Merry Pranksters, was connected with the Beats through Neal Cassady, the hero of *On the Road,* who drove the bus on their adventures in imitation of the *On the Road* road trips. As awareness of the Beats grew, other imitators appeared and their imitation lifestyle was variously promoted or ridiculed in the mass media. Combining *Beat* with *Sputnik*, the Russian satellite which was the first ever in space, they called themselves Beatniks and wanted to be as "far out" as the satellite. Eventually the label became *hippie* as the counterculture of the 1960s arrived, inspired to a great extent by the Beats, who lived their lives as spontaneously as they wrote.

Tonkinson goes on to write about Kerouac's last years:

> Amid hostility from the scions of the literary establishment, outrageous demands from a reading public that gave him no privacy, and a rising tide of "beatniks" who had less and less to do with Kerouac's beatific vision, he sank into alcoholic despair. Only a few years after their initial meeting, Kerouac wrote to Snyder that his Buddhism was dead. In his later years he turned toward the Catholic faith in which he was raised and continued to shy away from publicity, becoming more isolated even from his friends. (27)

Neither Kerouac nor his Beat friends and colleagues accepted the values of the dominant society that they had been raised in. The Beats marginalized themselves in an attempt to change America, to locate the promise that America holds out, and their voices can still be heard from the periphery.

CHAPTER SIX: THE TWENTY-FIRST CENTURY

> *. . . the revolution . . . has not been completed,*
> *either here in the United States or in any other nation in the world.*
> —Henry A. Wallace

The Future

Writers of literature regularly invent the self in each character, and they challenge the reader to attend to different cultural milieus. Even though many writers must go to some trouble to understand the hegemonic language and culture in order to communicate their message, they do so; for examples, consider contemporary American minority women writers Ana Castillo, Sandra Cisneros, and Amy Tan, who include non-standard English in their writing. Therefore, the reader is expected to also go to some trouble to open his or her mind, to attend to historical contexts, to imagine a different way of looking at the world. Native American writers Louise Erdrich and Leslie Marmon Silko, for example, express the interconnectedness of all things. These writers have blurred boundaries and created a hybrid culture in their works. In this age of globalization, they suggest a solution to the margin-versus-center model of looking at the world. The boundaries between cultures can thus be successfully negotiated.

Language and literature are very important components of culture formation. The critical theories of feminism, gender studies, new historicism, multiculturalism, and even deconstruction lead us to a new view of the self, culture, and the world. Literary trends point to the invention of the self and the active participation of the reader in creating meaning from the written word. And

122

the globalization of culture that the world is now experiencing requires reinvention of both self and culture.

Readers have the ability to accomplish this reinvention without leaving their chairs. In addition, by requiring more and more interaction between the reader and the text, these writers are able to make an actual change in the world. As we reorient our sense of cultural identity and literary form, we must find a cultural and literary model that more closely resembles the new situation. Writers are the ones with the creativity to imagine a different way of viewing the world or interacting with the world. I propose a new model for the humanities in light of the importance of language and literature to culture and in light of recent critical theory and literary trends, coupled with the globalization of culture.

The Construction of Identity

Much has been written about the formation of identity, both communal and individual identity. Werner Sollors posits that the construction of identity works through differences and writes that literature is important in "naturalizing the modern process of ethnic dissociation" (290). Cultural differences are important in constructing the self, but multiple perspectives can blend these differences.

In many contemporary novels by American minority women writers, the characters, the selves, that they invent move from being an oppressed object to being a speaking subject who can work to change the community. For example, in Alice Walker's *The Color Purple*, a novel written in the form of epistles, it is her protagonist's access to writing that leads to her making such a move. Words become weapons for Maxine Hong Kingston's *The Woman Warrior*, who fights for her family with words literally cut into her back. One of Sandra Cisneros's protagonists, a young girl, is able to reinvent herself through words and subsequently is able to help others. American minority women writers invent characters who are doubly marginalized, first by being members of an ethnic minority group, and then by being female. They show how these doubly marginalized characters are able to use their facility with words to translate between cultures, and sometimes between generations. Because they are intimately familiar with the hegemony as well, they are able to offer more than one perspective. As well, Jeanne Rossier Smith, in her discussion of the trickster myth, sees the self as a multiple of perspectives, with the ability to see the world from many different angles.

The Role of Language and Literature

When one society conquers another, the language of the conquering nation always becomes the hegemonic language, and all are forced to speak it if they want to be heard. As I have pointed out at length elsewhere, the oppressed learn the language of the oppressor and use it to speak against the oppressor to attain independence (*The Voice of the Oppressed in the Language of the Oppressor*). Many writers, from former colonies and from ethnic minorities in the United States, have learned to appropriate the oppressor's language and turn it against the oppressor, much like Shakespeare's character Caliban does to his master Prospero in Shakespeare's *The Tempest* when he learns to curse his master in his master's language, as Eric Cheyfitz points out in *The Poetics of Imperialism* (164). Werner Sollors acknowledges the importance of literature in "sustaining feelings of belonging" even though political boundaries may emphasize territoriality (289).

Race as an idea permeates American literature, and Thomas F. Gossett warns that it cannot be ignored. He observes that Americans have been led to "re-evaluate some of their own attitudes" (445), since minorities have come to have a greater presence. As well, he attributes to this reevaluation both a middle class who are "more secure in their status and thus less subject to hatred of other groups" and a greater incidence of intermarriage (444). The children of these mixed marriages may provide a unique viewpoint, a new way to see the world, which we can find in the literature of writers from American ethnic minorities.

The Role of Critical Theory

As British imperialism fell apart at around the middle of the twentieth century and the American civil rights movement changed the United States in the 1960s, many previously oppressed peoples gained liberation from their oppressors. According to one critic, Larry McCaffery (Ousby 752), the postmodern period of American literature began with the assassination of John F. Kennedy in 1963. At about the same time, recent critical theory, especially feminist and gender theory, new historicism, multiculturalism, and deconstruction, came into practice.

It is not my purpose to ascribe any cause and effect between political and historical events and theories of reading literature, however remarkably close in time they may have appeared. But it is true that, as African colonies gained their independence and became nations and African Americans gained their rights as citizens, women created a second feminist movement in the United States. Soon the disabled demanded access to public arenas, schools began to "main-stream" students in special education, and homosexuals and lesbians demanded that discrimination be ended. At about the same time, the new historicist theory of reading literature caused scholars to move away from the formalist approaches to literature and to find relationships between the literature and the historical period that produced it; as well, the newly liberated and formerly oppressed made the concept of multiculturalism a reality. Even the practice of the deconstructionist approach to literature calls attention to peripheral and marginalized characters in emphasizing the meaning of a work of literature.

The Role of the Reader

Doris Sommer points to the "incompetent reader" who does not understand the cultural backgrounds of what he or she is reading but who will be forced to become competent in interpreting signals based in other cultures. As well, she writes that some texts are resistant to the reader's comprehension, and so the reader must be educated in how to read particular markings. Contemporary authors are explaining the cultural backgrounds of their works within their stories in order to help the reader to understand the greater significance behind the characters and the actions of their novels and stories. However, it is imperative for the reader to open his or her mind to new ways of thinking and new ways of looking at the world in order for this understanding to come about. Sandra Jamieson uses Toni Morrison as an example of an author who teaches the reader "how to understand [the story], and in so doing creates an interpretive community" (148). The members of this interpretive community become a model of a community "in which members learn to understand the consequences of their lives and accept responsibility for their privileges" (148), suggesting a self-liberation or self-transformation.

A New Model for the Humanities

Whether physically or mentally through literature or technology, leaving home, according to Seamus Deane, can teach us to be "at home everywhere" (367), and, with today's technology, we may easily leave home in a manner other than physical. New perspectives and new voices have recently been legitimized, and they point to a new multiculturalism, or globalization. In the United States, there has been "exponential growth in efforts to 'internationalize' higher education: projects to bring international perspectives into the undergraduate curriculum, promote study abroad, build academic partnerships with foreign

126

universities, and even create American-style campuses around the world" (Lovett A40). However, the recent White House Global Cultural Initiative proposes "collaboration, but only among entities within the United States" (Lovett A40). But our view must be broader. For example, first-hand knowledge of another culture through study abroad would go a long way toward greater understanding between cultures. And first-hand experience with the practices of another culture can provide further insights to a different worldview. While society invents the concepts of individual, ethnicity, nation, culture, and community, change always happens first in the mind of the individual, and it is those persons who have enough creativity to imagine a different way who bring about change.

Human Thought and Technology

Humans and their society are constantly changing. Human development and the development of human society are continuous. It is through the written word that we can discover the history of these changes, and as humans we are able to observe and reflect on our individual and collective development; we can make decisions based on these reflections, learn from the past, and anticipate our future. One understanding that comes from studying our history is that as human consciousness (awareness) develops, there has been a parallel growth in the technology of communication. After the introduction of written language, for example, the mind was no longer required to hold everything in its memory, from history and inventories to plans for the future. And after the invention of the movable type press, books, which had been scarce and expensive because of the time and cost involved in producing them, became easy to produce and therefore cheaper. The people, now being able to afford reading material, had a reason to learn to read, and did so. Johannes von Gutenberg, the inventor of the movable type, influenced the way our minds developed, until now almost all of our learning is done through the printed word. *Time* magazine named Gutenberg the millennium's most influential person because his invention changed history, and it changed the way we think. Our changing technology, which includes the instant communication that we now enjoy through email, text messaging, and social networking, may become the means by which we will change our way of thinking again; however, even these new modes of communication depend heavily on the written word.

Based on a study of the past, we can speculate that we will be able to change our way of thinking and understanding ourselves, others, and the rest of the world. We will be able to visualize a new place in the world for humans and for human society. The new technology which has produced a new culture in which humans communicate electronically has also provided a new unity within that culture. At the same time, shifts in national policy have catapulted the United States from a colony to a world power.

Wars and epidemics, labor unrest and Prohibition, suffrage of black men and suffrage of women, the Great Depression and the Dust Bowl, the Harlem Renaissance and Jim Crow, the Cold War and the Red Scare, social work and communism, immigration and assimilation, the civil rights movement and two feminist movements, the assassination of two Presidents and the first trip to the moon, debates over the formation of the literary canon, and United States imperialism are some of the events, ideas, and movements that belong to the twentieth century. Josephine G. Hendin writes about the immigrant struggle in the second half of the twentieth century in her introduction to *A Concise Companion to Postwar American Literature and Culture*, which she also edited. Hendin states that "postwar ethnic literatures illuminate the crossroads of historical continuity and historical displacement" (16). She points out that "cultural interpenetration has enabled a sense of modernity as the experience of multiversity" (16).

Hendin's volume reflects an "ongoing dialogue across genres and perspectives, a discourse filled with oppositions and inventive mediations between art and the times" (17). Finally, Hendin links the result of "9/11" to the variety of writing in the postwar United States; she writes that "postwar writing bears witness to the genius and imaginative richness of these troubled times" (18). It also serves and contributes to a global ideal: "the power of art to inspire recognitions and dialogues across culture" (18).

But the United States is still uncertain of its place in the world. During the last half of the twentieth century, the United States faced "three fundamental challenges" that had to be met, according to the Gilder and Lehrman Institute of American History's "Module 23: The End of the Twentieth Century." From the first challenge, a "crisis in political leadership," beginning as President Kennedy was assassinated, as civil rights laws were being enacted, and as protests against the war in Vietnam were mounting, and continuing through the 1970s as the second feminist movement was under way and as "lobbies and special interest groups grew in power," and then moving through the second challenge of "wrenching economic transformations," the "third challenge involved growing uncertainty over America's proper role in the world." Even though the United States had become a superpower in terms of its military might and on the strength of the dollar, its military no longer wages war, but attempts to mollify tribal chieftains in foreign lands that it is attempting to "liberate," and the Peoples Republic of China has become a major competitor in capitalism. Even though there is a "current trend for transnational history" (Spiegel qtd. in Winkler), as we come to "focus on the mixture of cultures, and on the movement of peoples . . . and an implicit emphasis on the strength of hybrid cultures," the president of the American Historical Association warns against giving up the postmodern view and "its attention to loss, fractured meaning, and instability" (Winkler).

It took the United States seventy-five years after the American Revolution before it started to develop a national literature. It took almost another two hundred years after the revolution for American literature to gain a respectable place in the company of other national literatures. During the one hundred years of the twentieth century, the United States of America searched for its place in the global community; the society of this country underwent many changes in its concept of humankind's place in the world as immigrants, minority groups, and women and other marginalized groups came to be heard; as well, literary writers fictionalized their own observations and experiences to help individuals find their identities as Americans. As the concept of "American" changed, both individuals and communities who wanted to be part of the American hegemony were forced to change with it. We can find much evidence in both American literature and American history that America and Americans are still becoming.

WORKS CITED

Abu-Jaber, Diana. *Arabian Jazz*. New York: Norton, 1993. Print.

---. *Crescent*. New York: Norton, 2003. Print.

Adams, Henry. "The Dynamo and the Virgin." *The American Intellectual Tradition: Volume II: 1865 to the Present*. Ed. David A. Hollinger and Charles Capper. Oxford: Oxford UP, 2006. 97-100. Print.

Almeida, Linda Dowling. "Irish America, 1940-2000." *Making the Irish American: History and Heritage of the Irish in the United States*. Ed. J. J. Lee and Marion R. Casey. New York: New York UP. 2006. 548-73. Print.

Antell, Judith A. "Momaday, Welch, and Silko: Expressing the Feminine Principle through Male Alienation." *American Indian Quarterly* 12.3 (1988): 213-20. JSTOR. Web. 21 Dec. 2009.

Antler, Joyce. "Between Culture and Politics: The Emma Lazarus Federation of Jewish Women's Clubs and the Promulgation of Women's History." *U. S. History as Women's History: New Feminist Essays*. Ed. Linda K. Kerber, Alice Kessler-Harris, and Kathryn Kish Sklar. Chapel Hill: U of North Carolina P, 1993. 267-95. Print.

Ashcroft, Bill, Gareth Griffiths, and Helen Tiffin. *The Empire Writes Back: Theory and Practice in Post-colonial Literatures*. London: Routledge, 1989. Print.

---. *Post-Colonial Studies: The Key Concepts*. London: Routledge, 2000. Print.

Associated Press. "Nobel Chief Disparages U.S. as 'Too Insular' for Great Writing." *The Washington Post*. October 1, 2008. Web. 7 October 2010.

Aubrey, James R. "Woman Warriors and Military Students." *Approaches to Teaching Kingston's* The Woman Warrior. Ed. Shirley Geok-lin Lim. New York: MLA, 1991. 80-86. Print.

Baker, Charles. *William Faulkner's Postcolonial South*. Modern American Literature: New Approaches Ser. Yoshinobu Hakutani, general ed. New York: Peter Lang, 2000. Print.

Baldwin, James. "Many Thousand Gone." *The American Intellectual Tradition: Volume II: 1865 to the Present*. Ed. David A. Hollinger and Charles Capper. Oxford: Oxford UP, 2006. 314-23. Print.

Baym, Nina. *Feminism and American Literary History*. New Brunswick, N. J.: Rutgers UP, 1992. Print.

---, et al., eds. "Flannery O'Connor." *The Norton Anthology of American Literature*. Vol. 2, 4th ed. New York: Norton, 1994. 2093-94. Print.

Beardslee, Karen E. *Literary Legacies, Folklore Foundations: Selfhood and Cultural Tradition in Nineteenth- and Twentieth-Century American Literature*. Knoxville: U of Tennessee P, 2001. Print.

Beer, Robert. *The Handbook of Tibetan Buddhist Symbols*. Serindia Publications, 2003. Web. 20 December 2007.

Bernstein, Charles. "What's Art Got to Do with It? The Status of the Subject of the Humanities in the Age of Cultural Studies." *The American Literary History Reader*. Ed. Gordon Hutner. New York: Oxford UP, 1995. 370-87. Print.

Blum, John Morton. *Years of Discord: American Politics and Society, 1961-1974*. New York: Norton, 1991. Print.

Bourne, Randolph. "Trans-National America." *The American Intellectual Tradition: Volume II: 1865 to the Present*. Ed. David A. Hollinger and Charles Capper. Oxford: Oxford UP, 2006. 170-80. Print.

Bradbury, Malcolm. *The Modern American Novel*. Oxford: Oxford UP, 1984. Print.

Brown, Nikki L. "War Work, Social Work, Community Work: Alice Dunbar-Nelson, Federal War Work Agencies, and Southern African American Women." *Post-Bellum, Pre-Harlem: African American Literature and Culture, 1877-1919*. Ed. Barbara McCaskill and Caroline Gebhard. New York: New York UP, 2006. 197-209. Print.

Bryant, J. A., Jr. *Twentieth Century Southern Literature*. Lexington: UP of Kentucky, 1997. Print.

Casey, Daniel J., and Robert E. Rhodes. "The Tradition of Irish-American Writers: The Twentieth Century." *Making the Irish American: History and Heritage of the Irish in the United States*. Ed. J. J. Lee and Marion R. Casey. New York: New York UP. 2006. 649-62. Print.

Chodorow, Nancy J. "Gender, Relation, and Difference in Psychoanalytic Perspective." *Feminism and Psychoanalytic Theory*. Ed. Nancy J. Chodorow. New Haven: Yale UP, 1979. 99-113. Rpt. *The American Intellectual Tradition: Volume II: 1865 to the Present*. Ed. David A. Hollinger and Charles Capper. Oxford: Oxford UP, 2006. 476-87. Print.

---, with Susan Contratto. "The Fantasy of the Perfect Mother." *Feminism and Psychoanalytic Theory*. Ed. Nancy J. Chodorow. New Haven: Yale UP, 1989. 79-96. Print.

Chomsky, Noam. "The Responsibility of Intellectuals." *The American Intellectual Tradition: Volume II: 1865 to the Present.* Ed. David A. Hollinger and Charles Capper. Oxford: Oxford UP, 2006. 455-64. Print.

Chua, Cheng Lok. "Mythopoesis East and West in *The Woman Warrior.*" *Approaches to Teaching Kingston's* The Woman Warrior. Ed. Shirley Geok-lin Lim. New York: MLA, 1991. 146-50. Print.

Cooper, John Milton, Jr. *Pivotal Decades: The United States, 1900-1920.* New York: Norton, 1990. Print.

Dardess, George. "The Delicate Dynamics of Friendship: A Reconsideration of Kerouac's *On the Road.*" *American Literature: A Journal of Literary History, Criticism, and Bibliography* 46.2 (May 1974): 200-06. MLA International Bibliography database, Academic Search Premier. Web. 8 December 2007.

Davidson, Cathy N. *Revolution and the Word: The Rise of the Novel in America.* Expanded ed. Oxford: Oxford UP, 2004. Print.

Dawahare, Anthony. "The Spector of Radicalism in Alain Locke's *The New Negro.*" *Left of the Color Line: Race, Radicalism, and Twentieth-Century Literature of the United States.* Ed. Bill V. Mullen and James Smethurst. Chapel Hill: U of North Carolina P, 2003. 68-85. Print.

Deane, Seamus. "Imperialism/Nationalism." *Critical Terms for Literary Study.* 2nd ed. Ed. Frank Lentricchia and Thomas McLaughlin. Chicago: U of Chicago P, 1995. 354-68. Print.

De Hart, Jane Sherron. "Rights and Representation: Women, Politics, and Power in the Contemporary United States." *U. S. History as Women's History: New Feminist Essays.* Ed. Linda K. Kerber, Alice Kessler-Harris, and Kathryn Kish Sklar. Chapel Hill: U of North Carolina P, 1993. 214-42. Print.

Delbanco, Andrew. "The Decline and Fall of Literature." *The New York Review of Books* 46.17 (November 4, 1999). Web. 3 August 2008.

Diggins, John Patrick. *The Proud Decades: America in War and Peace, 1941-1960.* New York: Norton, 1988. Print.

Dorris, Michael. "Native American Literature in an Ethnohistorical Context." *College English* 41.2 (1979): 147-62. JSTOR. Web. 12 April 2008.

Du Bois, W. E. B. "Selection from *The Souls of Black Folk.*" *The American Intellectual Tradition: Volume II: 1865 to the Present.* Ed. David A. Hollinger and Charles Capper. Oxford: Oxford UP, 2006. 148-53. Print.

Eagleton, Terry. *Literary Theory: An Introduction.* Minneapolis, U of Minnesota P, 1983. Print.

Elfenbein, Anna Shannon. "A Forgotten Revolutionary Voice: 'Woman's Place' and Race in Olive Dargan's *Call Home the Heart*." *The Female Tradition in Southern Literature*. Ed. Carol S. Manning. Urbana: U of Illinois P, 1993. Print.

Ellis, John M. *Literature Lost: Social Agendas and the Corruption of the Humanities*. New Haven: Yale UP, 1997. Print.

Ellison, Ralph. *Shadow & Act*. New York: Signet, 1953.

Ferraro, Thomas J. *Ethnic Passages: Literary Immigrants in Twentieth-Century America*. Chicago: U of Chicago P, 1993. Print.

Fiedler, Leslie A. *Love and Death in the American Novel*. New York: Criterion, 1960. Print.

Foertsch, Jacqueline. *American Culture in the 1940s*. Twentieth-Century American Culture Ser. Martin Halliwell, general ed. Edinburgh: Edinburgh UP, 2008. Print.

Friere, Paulo. *Pedagogy of the Oppressed*. New York: Continuum, 1993. Print.

Gates, Henry Louis, Jr. *Loose Canons: Notes on the Culture Wars*. Oxford: Oxford UP, 1993. Print.

Gilder Lehrman Institute of American History. *America at the End of the Twentieth Century*. "Module 23: The End of the Twentieth Century." Web. 18 January 2010.

Ginsberg, Allen. "Notes Written on Finally Recording 'Howl'." Web. 18 March 2007.

---. Introduction. *First Thought Best Thought: 108 Poems*. Chögyam Trungpa. Boulder, Colo.: Shambhala, 1983. xi-xviii. Print.

Global Oneness Commitment. "Nirmanakaya." Web. 20 December 2007.

Gonzales, Marcial. "A Marxist Critique of Borderlands Postmodernism: Adorno's *Negative Dialectics* and Chicano Cultural Criticism." *Left of the Color Line: Race, Radicalism, and Twentieth-Century Literature of the United States*. Ed. Bill Mullen and James Smethurst. Chapel Hill: U of North Carolina P, 2003. 279-97. Print.

Gossett, Thomas. *Race: The History of an Idea in America*. New ed. Oxford: Oxford UP, 1997. Print.

Gutiérrez, Ramón, and Genaro Padilla, eds. *Recovering the U. S. Hispanic Literary Heritage*. Houston: Arte Publico Press, 1993. Print.

Habermas, Jürgen. *The Structural Transformation of the Public Sphere: An Inquiry into a Category of Bourgeois Society*. Cambridge: MIT P, 1991. Print.

Halliwell, Martin. *American Culture in the 1950s.* Twentieth-Century American Culture Ser. Martin Halliwell, general ed. Edinburgh: Edinburgh UP, 2007. Print.

Hart, James D. "O'Connor, Flannery." *The Oxford Companion to American Literature.* 6th ed. Ed. James D. Hart. New York: Oxford UP, 1995. 483. Print.

Harte, Bret. "The Rise of the 'Short Story'." *The American Short Story and its Writer.* Ed. Ann Charters. Boston: Bedford / St. Martin's, 2000. 1356-62. Print.

Hendin, Josephine G. "Introducing American Literature and Culture in the Postwar Years." *A Concise Companion to Postwar American Literature and Culture.* Ed. Josephine G. Hendin. Malden, Mass.: Blackwell, 2004. 1-19. Print.

Hill, Laban Carrick. *Harlem Stomp! A Cultural History of the Harlem Renaissance.* New York: Little, Brown, 2003. Print.

Hinojosa-Smith, Rolando. Foreword. *Hispanic American Literature: An Anthology.* Ed. Rodolfo Cortina. Lincolnwood, Ill.: NTC, 1998. xi. Print.

Ho, Fred. "Bamboo That Snaps Back! Resistance and Revolution in Asian Pacific American Working-Class and Left-Wing Expressive Culture." *Left of the Color Line: Race, Radicalism, and Twentieth-Century Literature of the United States.* Ed. Bill V. Mullen and James Smethurst. Chapel Hill: U of North Carolina P, 2003. 239-58. Print.

Hollinger, David A., and Charles Capper, eds. *The American Intellectual Tradition: Volume II: 1865 to the Present.* Oxford: Oxford UP, 2006.

Howard, Jennifer. "In Jefferson Lecture, Updike Says American Art Is Known by Its Insecurity." *The Chronicle of Higher Education* News Blog May 23, 2008. Web. 26 May 2008.

Huda. "Crescent Moon: Symbol of Islam?" January 2005. Web.

Hutner, Gordon, ed. *The American Literary History Reader.* New York: Oxford UP, 1995. Print.

Jameson, Fredric. "Modernism and Imperialism." *Nationalism, Colonialism, and Literature.* Terry Eagleton, Fredric Jameson, and Edward Said. Minneapolis: Minnesota UP, 1990. 43-66. Print.

Jamieson, Sandra. "Text, Context, and Teaching Literature by African American Women." *Understanding Others: Cultural and Cross-Cultural Studies and the Teaching of Literature.* Ed. Joseph Trimmer and Tilly Warnock. Urbana: NCTE, 1992. 139-52. Print.

Jen, Gish. *Typical American.* New York: Vintage, 2008. Print.

136

Johnson, Haynes. *Sleepwalking Through History: America in the Reagan Years.*
    New York: Norton, 2003. Print.
Jurca, Catherine. *White Diaspora: The Suburb and the Twentieth Century
    American Novel.* Princeton: Princeton UP, 2001. Print.
Karl, Frederick R. "The Fifties and After: An Ambiguous Culture." *A Concise
    Companion to Postwar American Literature and Culture.* Ed. Josephine
    G. Hendin. Malden, Mass.: Blackwell, 2004. 20-71. Print.
Kazin, Alfred. *On Native Grounds: An Interpretation of Modern American
    Prose Literature.* New York: Reynal & Hitchcock, 1942. Print.
Kenny, Kevin. "American-Irish Nationalism." *Making the Irish American:
    History and Heritage of the Irish in the United States.* Ed. J. J. Lee and
    Marion R. Casey. New York: New York UP, 2006. 289-301. Print.
Kerouac, Jack. "Belief & Technique for Modern Prose." Web. 18 March 2007.
---. "Essentials of Spontaneous Prose." Web. 18 March 2007.
---. *On the Road.* New York: Penguin, 1957. Print.
---. "Wake Up." *Tricycle: The Buddhist Review* II.4 (Summer 1993): 12-17.
    Print.
khandro.net. "Trikaya." Web. 20 December 2007.
Kim, Janine Young. "Are Asians Black?" *Contemporary Asian America: A
    Multidisciplinary Reader.* Ed. Min Zhou and J. V. Gatewood. New York:
    New York UP, 2007. 331-53. Print.
Kingston, Maxine Hong. *The Fifth Book of Peace.* New York: Knopf, 2003.
    Print.
---. *The Woman Warrior: Memoirs of a Girlhood Among Ghosts.* 1976. New
    York: Vintage, 1989. Print.
---. *Tripmaster Monkey: His Fake Book.* 1987. New York: Vintage, 1990. Print.
Lee, Jennifer, and Frank D. Bean. "Intermarriage and Multiracial Identification."
    Contemporary Asian America: A Multidisciplinary Reader. Ed. Min Zhou
    and J. V. Gatewood. New York: New York UP, 2007. 381-92. Print.
Levine, George. "Introduction: Constructivism and the Reemergent Self."
    Constructions of the Self. New Brunswick: Rutgers UP, 1992. Print.
Lovett, Clara M. "We Need a New Model of Global Education." Commentary.
    The Chronicle of Higher Education 54.31 (April 11, 2008): A40. Print.
Luce, Henry R. "Selection from 'The American Century'." *The American
    Intellectual Tradition: Volume II: 1865 to the Present.* Ed. David A.
    Hollinger and Charles Capper. Oxford: Oxford UP, 2006. 260-64. Print.
Lynch-Brennan, Margaret. "Ubiquitous Bridget: Irish Immigrant Women in
    Domestic Service in America, 1840-1930." *Making the Irish American:*

History and Heritage of the Irish in the United States. Ed. J. J. Lee and Marion R. Casey. New York: New York UP. 2006. 332-53. Print.

Maeda, Daryl J. "Black Panthers, Red Guards, and Chinamen." *Contemporary Asian America: A Multidisciplinary Reader.* Ed. Min Zhou and J. V. Gatewood. New York: New York UP, 2007. 89-109. Print.

Manning, Carol S. "The Real Beginning of the Southern Renaissance." *The Female Tradition in Southern Literature.* Ed. Carol S. Manning. Urbana: U of Illinois P, 1993. 37-56. Print.

Mark, Gary T. "The White Negro and the Negro White." *Phylon* 28.2 (1967): 168-77. Print.

McGann, Jerome J. "Introduction: A Point of Reference." *Historical Studies and Literary Criticism.* Ed. Jerome J. McGann. U of Wisconsin P, 1985. 3-21. Print.

Medovoi, Leerom. *Rebels: Youth and the Cold War Origins of Identity.* Durham: Duke UP, 2005. Print.

Monteith, Sharon. *American Culture in the 1960s.* Twentieth-Century American Culture Ser. Martin Halliwell, general ed. Edinburgh: Edinburgh UP, 2008. Print.

Moynihan, Daniel Patrick. "The Irish." *Making the Irish American: History and Heritage of the Irish in the United States.* Ed. J. J. Lee and Marion R. Casey. New York: New York UP. 2006, 475-525. Print.

Mullen, Bill V., and James Smethurst. Introduction. *Left of the Color Line: Race, Radicalism, and Twentieth-Century Literature of the United States.* Ed. Bill Mullen and James Smethurst. Chapel Hill: U of North Carolina P, 2003. 1-12. Print.

Myrdal, Gunnar. "Selection from *An American Dilemma: The Negro Problem and American Democracy.*" *The American Intellectual Tradition: Volume II: 1865 to the Present.* Ed. David A. Hollinger and Charles Capper. Oxford: Oxford UP, 2006. 270-78. Print.

O'Connor, Flannery. "The Life You Save May Be Your Own." *The Norton Anthology of American Literature.* Vol. 2, 4th ed. Ed. Nina Baym, et al. New York: Norton, 1994. 2094-102. Print.

---. "Good Country People." *The Norton Anthology of American Literature.* Vol. 2, 4th ed. Ed. Nina Baym, et al. New York: Norton, 1994. 2102-16. Print.

"O'Connor, Flannery." *Merriam Webster's Encyclopedia of Literature.* Springfield, Mass.: Merriam-Webster, 1995. 824. Print.

O'Connor, Margaret Anne. "O'Connor, Flannery." *The Oxford Companion to Women's Writing in the United States.* Ed. Cathy N. Davidson and Linda Wagner Martin. New York: Oxford UP, 1995. 641 42. Print.

Ousby, Ian, ed. "Post-modernism." *The Cambridge Guide to Literature in English.* New ed. Cambridge, England: Cambridge UP, 1993. 752. Print.

Owens, Louis. *Other Destinies: Understanding the American Indian Novel.* American Indian Literature and Cultural Studies Ser. Gerald Vizenor, general ed. Norman: U of Oklahoma P, 1992. Print.

Paredes, Américo. "The Folk Base of Chicano Literature." *Modern Chicano Writers: A Collection of Critical Essays.* Ed. Joseph Sommers and Tomás Ybarra-Frausto. Englewood Clifs, N. J.: Prentice-Hall. 1979. 4-17. Print.

Parrish, Michael E. *Anxious Decades: America in Prosperity and Depression, 1920-1941.* New York: Norton, 1992. Print.

"Postmodern." *Merriam-Webster's Encyclopedia of Literature.* Springfield, Mass.: Merriam-Webster, 1995. 899. Print.

Prothero, Stephen. Introduction. *Big Sky Mind: Buddhism and the Beat Generation.* Ed. Carole Tonkinson. New York: Riverhead, 1995. 1-22. Print.

Randall, Willard Sterne. *Thomas Jefferson: A Life.* New York: HarperCollins, 1994. Print.

Renker, Elizabeth. *The Origins of American Literature Studies: An Institutional History.* Cambridge: Cambridge UP, 2007. Print.

Reynolds, David S. *Beneath the American Renaissance: The Subversive Imagination in the Age of Emerson and Melville.* New York: Knopf, 1988. Print.

Rodriguez, Richard. *Days of Obligation: An Argument with My Mexican Father.* New York: Penguin, 1993. Print.

Roediger, David R. *Working Toward Whiteness: How America's Immigrants Became White: The Strange Journey from Ellis Island to the Suburbs.* New York: Basic, 2005. Print.

Ruiz, Ramón E. Introduction: "On the Meaning of Pocho." *Pocho.* 1959. José Antonio Villarreal. Garden City, N. Y.: Anchor, 1970. vii-xii. Print.

Sampas, John. Untitled comment. *Tricycle: The Buddhist Review* II.4 (Summer 1993): 12. Print.

Sandler, Lauren. "Iraq's Women: Occupied Territory." *Amnesty Now.* New York: Amnesty International, Winter 2003. 22-26. Print.

Schueller, Malini Johar. *U. S. Orientalisms: Race, Nation, and Gender in Literature, 1790-1800.* Ann Arbor: UP of Michigan, 1998.

---, and Edward Watts. "Introduction: Theorizing Early American Studies and Postcoloniality." *Messy Beginnings: Postcoloniality and Early American Studies.* Ed. Malina Johar Schueller and Edward Watts. New Brunswick, N. J.: Rutgers UP, 2003.

Simmen, Edward. Preface and Introduction. *The Chicano: From Caricature to Self-Portrait.* Ed. Edward Simmen. New York: New American Library, 1971. xi-xiv, 15-26. Print.

Sollors, Werner. "Ethnicity." *Critical Terms for Literary Study.* 2nd ed. Ed. Frank Lentricchia and Thomas McLaughlin. Chicago: U of Chicago P, 1995. 288-305. Print.

Sommer, Doris. "Resistant Texts and Incompetent Readers." *Poetics Today* 15 (1994): 523-52. Print.

Subramanian, Ajantha. "Indians in North Carolina." *Contemporary Asian America: A Multidisciplinary Reader.* Ed. Min Zhou and J. V. Gatewood. New York: New York UP, 2007. 158-75. Print.

Sulieman, Michael W. "Introduction: The Arab Immigrant Experience." *Arabs in America: Building a New Future.* Ed. Michael W. Suleiman. Philadelphia: Temple UP, 1999. 1-21. Print.

Swerdlow, Amy. "The Congress of American Women: Left-Feminist Peace Politics in the Cold War." *U. S. History as Women's History: New Feminist Essays.* Ed. Linda K. Kerber, Alice Kessler-Harris, and Kathryn Kish Sklars. Chapel Hill: U of North Carolina P, 1993. 296-312. Print.

Thompson, Graham. *American Culture in the 1980s.* Twentieth-Century American Culture Ser. Martin Halliwell, general ed. Edinburgh: Edinburgh UP, 2007. Print.

Tiffin, Helen. "Post-Colonial Literatures and Counter-Discourse." *The Post-Colonial Studies Reader.* Ed. Bill Ashcroft, Gareth Griffiths, and Helen Tiffin. London: Routledge, 1995. 95-98. Print.

Tompkins, Jane. *Sensational Designs: The Cultural Work of American Fiction, 1790-1860.* New York: Oxford UP, 1985. Print.

Tonkinson, Carole, ed. *Big Sky Mind: Buddhism and the Beat Generation.* New York: Riverhead, 1995.

Trungpa, Chögyam. *Shambhala: The Sacred Path of the Warrior.* Boulder: Shambhala, 1984. Print.

Tyson, Lois. *Critical Theory Today: A User-Friendly Guide.* 2nd ed. New York: Routledge, 2006.

Umemoto, Karen. "On Strike!" *Contemporary Asian America: A Multidisciplinary Reader.* Ed. Min Zhou and J. V. Gatewood. New York: New York UP, 2007. 25-55. Print.

Vizenor, Gerald. *Dead Voices: Natural Agonies in the New World.* Norman: U of Oklahoma P, 1992. Print.

Wallace, Henry A. "Selection from *The Century of the Common Man.*" New York, 1943. Rpt. *The American Intellectual Tradition: Volume II: 1865 to the Present.* Ed. David A. Hollinger and Charles Capper. Oxford: Oxford UP, 2006. 265-69. Print.

Washington, Mary Helen. "Alice Childress, Lorraine Hansberry, and Claudia Jones: Black Women Write the Popular Front." *Left of the Color Line: Race, Radicalism, and Twentieth-Century Literature of the United States.* Ed. Bill V. Mullen and James Smethurst. Chapel Hill: U of North Carolina P, 2003. 181-205.

Watson, Steven. *The Birth of the Beat Generation: Visionaries, Rebels, and Hipsters, 1944-1960.* New York: Pantheon, 1995. Print.

Weinreich, Regina. "The Beat Generation Is Now About Everything." *A Concise Companion to Postwar American Literature and Culture.* Josephine G. Hendin, ed. Malden, Mass.: Blackwell, 2004. 2-94. Print.

Wilson, Steve. "'Buddha Writing': The Author and the Search for Authenticity in Jack Kerouac's *On the Road* and *The Subterraneans.*" *Midwest Quarterly: A Journal of Contemporary Thought* 40.3 (Spring 1999): 302-15. MLA International Bibliography database, Academic Search Premier. Web. 8 December 2007.

Wilson, Woodrow. "The Ideals of America." *The American Intellectual Tradition: Volume II: 1865 to the Present.* Ed. David A. Hollinger and Charles Capper. Oxford: Oxford UP, 2006. 140-47. Print.

Winkler, Karen J. "After Postmodernism: A Historian Reflects on Where the Field Is Going." *The Chronicle of Higher Education* News Blog. Web. 4 January 2009.

Wright, Richard. *Native Son.* 1940. New York: HarperPerennial, 1997. Print.

Zhou, Min. "Are Asian Americans Becoming White?" *Contemporary Asian America: A Multidisciplinary Reader.* Ed. Min Zhou and J. V. Gatewood. New York: New York UP, 2007. 354-59. Print.

141

---, and J. V. Gatewood. Preface to the Second Edition. *Contemporary Asian America: A Multidisciplinary Reader.* 2nd ed. Ed. Min Zhou and J. V. Gatewood. New York: New York UP, 2007. Print.

Zinn, Howard. *The Twentieth Century: A People's History.* From the author's *A People's History of the United States.* New York: Harper Perennial, 2003. Print.

WORKS CONSULTED

Achebe, Chinua. "An Image of Africa: Racism in Conrad's *Heart of Darkness.*" *Massachusetts Review* 18 (1977): 782-94. Rpt. Robert Kimbrough, ed. *Heart of Darkness.* Joseph Conrad. Norton Critical ed. 3rd ed. New York: Norton, 1988. 251-62. Print.

---. *Things Fall Apart.* 1959. New York: Anchor Books, 1994. Print.

Anderson, Sherwood. *Winesburg, Ohio. Sherwood Anderson's* Winesburg, Ohio*: Text and Criticism.* Ed. John H. Ferres. Viking Critical Ser. New York: Penguin, 1977. 23-247. Print.

Bardes, Barbara A., and Suzanne Gossett, eds. "Catharine Maria Sedgwick (1789-1867)." Cengage. Web.13 June 2010.

"Bernal Diaz del Castillo." Nina Baym, et al. *The Norton Anthology of American Literature* Vol 1, 4th ed. Ed. Nina Baym, et al. New York: Norton, 1994. 24. Print.

Bhabha, Homi. "The Commitment to Theory." *The Location of Culture.* Homi Bhabha. London: Routledge, 2004. 19-39. Print.

Bradstreet, Anne. *The Heath Anthology of American Literature.* Vol. 1, 4th ed. Ed. Paul Lauter. Boston: Houghton Mifflin, 2002. 382-401.

Brooks, Cleanth. *The Well-Wrought Urn: Studies in the Structure of Poetry.* New York: Harcourt Brace, 1947. Print.

Bray, Paul. "William Cullen Bryant." *Encyclopedia of American Poetry: The Nineteenth Century.* Ed. Eric L. Haralson. New York: Routledge, 1998. 57-61. Print.

"Captain John Smith." *The Harper Single Volume American Literature* 3rd ed. Donald McQuade, general ed. New York: Longman, 1999. 55-56. Print.

Castillo, Ana. *So Far From God: A Novel.* New York: Plume, 1993. Print.

Cheyfitz, Eric. *The Poetics of Imperialism: Translation and Colonization from* The Tempest *to* Tarzan. Expanded ed. Philadelphia: U of Pennsylvania P, 1997. Print.

Cisneros, Sandra. *The House on Mango Street.* 1984. New York: Vintage Books, 1991. Print.

"Cooper, James Fenimore." Mohican Press. Web. 13 June 2010.

Crane, Stephen. *Maggie, a Girl of the Streets.* Norton Critical ed. Ed. Thomas A. Gullason. New York: Norton, 1979. 1-58. Print.

---. "The Open Boat." *Literature: An Introduction to Fiction, Poetry, Drama, and Writing.* 10th ed. Ed. X. J. Kennedy and Dana Gioia. New York: Pearson Longman, 2007. 191-207. Print.

de Perucker, G. "Dharmakaya." *The Occult Glossary.* Theosophical UP, 1996. Web. 20 December 2007.

---. "Nirmanakaya." *The Occult Glossary.* Theosophical UP, 1996. Web. 20 December 2007.

---. "Samboghakaya." *The Occult Glossary.* Theosophical UP, 1996. Web. 20 December 2007.

Daniels, Patsy J. *The Voice of the Oppressed in the Language of the Oppressor.* Literary Criticism and Cultural Theory Ser. William E. Cain, general ed. New York: Routledge, 2001. Print.

Edwards, Jonathan. "Sinners in the Hands of an Angry God." *The Norton Anthology of American Literature.* Vol. 1, 4th ed. Ed. Nina Baym, et al. New York: Norton, 1994. 412-23. Print.

Erdrich, Louise. *Love Medicine.* New and expanded version. New York: HarperPerennial, 1993. Print.

Fanon, Frantz. *The Wretched of the Earth.* Trans. Richard Philcox. New York: Grove, 2004. Print.

Faulkner, William. "A Rose for Emily." *Literature: An Introduction to Fiction, Poetry, Drama, and Writing.* 10th ed. Ed. X. J. Kennedy and Dana Gioia. New York: Pearson Longman, 2007. 28-34. Print.

---. "Barn Burning." *Literature: An Introduction to Fiction, Poetry, Drama, and Writing.* 10th ed. Ed. X. J. Kennedy and Dana Gioia. New York: Pearson Longman, 2007. 160-72. Print.

Geertz, Clifford. "Thick Description: Toward an Interpretive Theory of Culture." *The Interpretation of Cultures: Selected Essays.* New York: Basic Books, 1973. 3-30. Print.

Hawthorne, Nathaniel. "The Custom House." *The Portable Hawthorne.* Revised and expanded ed. Ed. Malcolm Cowley. New York: Viking, 1969. 293-337. Print.

Irving, Washington. *The Sketchbook of Geoffery Crayon, Gent.* 1819-1820. New York: Signet, 2010. Print.

Katznelson, Ira. *When Affirmative Action Was White: An Untold History of Racial Inequality in Twentieth-Century America.* New York: Norton, 2005. Print.

Kerber, Linda K., Alice Kessler-Harris, and Kathryn Kish Sklar, eds. *U. S. History as Women's History: New Feminist Essays.* Chapel Hill: U of North Carolina P, 1993. 313-34. Print.

Leitch, Vincent B., general ed. *The Norton Anthology of Theory and Criticism.* New York: Norton, 2001. Print.

London, Jack. *The Call of the Wild.* 1903. New York: MacMillan, 1912. Print.

"Négritude." *Encyclopedia Britannica.* Web. 25 July 2010.

Norris, Frank. "A Deal in Wheat." *Selected American Prose, 1841-1900: The Realistic Movement.* Ed. Wallace Stegner. New York: Holt, Rinehart and Winston, 1958. 216-27.

Plato. *The Republic and Other Works.* Trans. B. Jowett. New York: Anchor, 1973. Print.

Poe, Edgar Allan. "Manuscript Found in a Bottle." 1833. Web.1 August 2008.

Porter, Katherine Anne. "The Fig Tree." *The Norton Anthology of American Literature* Vol. 2, 4th ed. Ed. Nina Baym, et al. New York: Norton, 1994. 1408-15. Print.

Rosen, Ruth. "The Female Generation Gap: Daughters of the Fifties and the Origins of Contemporary American Feminism." *U. S. History as Women's History: New Feminist Essays.* Ed. Linda K. Kerber, Alice Kessler-Harris, and Kathryn Kish Sklar. Chapel Hill: U of North Carolina P, 1993. 313-34. Print.

Roth, Phillip. *Good-bye, Columbus. Seven Contemporary Short Novels.* 3rd ed. Ed. Charles Clerc and Louis Leiter. New York: Harper Collins, 1982. 1-96. Print.

Rowlandson, Mary. "Narrative of the Captivity and Restoration of Mrs. Mary Rowlandson." 1682. *The Norton Anthology of American Literature* Vol. 1, 4th ed. Ed. Nina Baym et al. New York: Norton, 1994. 244-75. Print.

Said, Edward W. "Selection from *Orientalism.*" *The American Intellectual Tradition: Volume II: 1865 to the Present.* Ed. David A. Hollinger and Charles Capper. Oxford: Oxford UP, 2006. 465-75. Print.

Silberman, Steve. "Impossible Happiness: Steve Silberman's Elegy for Peter Orlovsky." *Shambala Sun* 19.1 (Sept. 2010): 33-37. Print.

Silko, Leslie Marmon. "Lullaby." *The Harper Single Volume American Literature* 3rd ed. Donald McQuade, general ed. New York: Longman, 1999. 2663-68. Print.

Smethurst, James Edward. *The Black Arts Movement: Literary Nationalism in the 1960s and 1970s.* Chapel Hill: U of North Carolina P, 2005. Print.

Smith, Jeanne Rossier. *Writing Tricksters: Mythic Gambols in American Ethnic Literature.* Berkeley: U of California P, 1997. Print.

Spivak, Gayatri Chakravorty. *In Other Worlds: Essays in Cultural Politics.* New York: Routledge, 1998. Print.

Stein, Gertrude. *Three Lives.* 1909. New York: Vintage, 1936. Print.

Stephens, Mitchell. "Jürgen Habermas: The Theologian of Talk." *Los Angeles Times Magazine.* October 23,1994. Web. 5 August 2010.

Stowe, Harriet Beecher. *Uncle Tom's Cabin.* 1852. 2nd Norton Critical ed. Ed. Elizabeth Ammons. New York: Norton, 2010. Print.

Tan, Amy. *The Joy Luck Club.* New York: Ivy Books, 1989. Print.

Thiong'o, Ngugi wă, Taban lo Liyong, and Henry Owuor-Anyumba. "On the Abolition of the English Department." 1968. *The Post-Colonial Studies Reader.* Ed. Bill Ashcroft, Gareth Griffiths, and Helen Tiffin. London: Routledge, 1995. 438-42. Print.

Trilling, Lionel. "On the Teaching of Modern Literature." *Beyond Culture.* New York: Harcourt Brace Jovanovitch, 1961. 3-27. Rpt. *The American Intellectual Tradition: Volume II: 1865 to the Present.* Ed. David A. Hollinger and Charles Capper. Oxford: Oxford UP, 2006. 376-89. Print.

Twain, Mark. *Adventures of Huckleberry Finn. A Case Study in Critical Controversy.* Ed. Gerald Graff and James Phelan. Boston: Bedford St. Martin's, 1995. 27-265. Print.

Vonnegut, Kurt, Jr. *Slaughterhouse-Five. Seven Contemporary Short Novels.* 3rd ed. Ed. Charles Clerc and Louis Leiter. New York: Harper Collins, 1982. 161-291. Print.

Walker, Alice. *The Color Purple.* New York: Pocket Books, 1982. Print.

Wall, Cheryl A. *Worrying the Line: Black Women Writers, Lineage, and Literary Tradition.* Chapel Hill: U of North Carolina P. 2005.

Weinreich, Regina. *Kerouac's Spontaneous Prose: A Study of the Fiction.* New York: Thunder's Mouth, 1987.

Welty, Eudora. "A Worn Path." *Literature: An Introduction to Fiction, Poetry, Drama, and Writing.* 10th ed. Ed. X. J. Kennedy and Dana Gioia. New York: Pearson Longman, 2007. 64-69. Print.

Wright, Richard. "Almos' a Man." *The Best Short Stories by Negro Writers: An Anthology from 1899 to the Present.* Ed. Langston Hughes. Boston: Little, Brown, 1967. 91-103. Print.

INDEX

148

152

154

158

160

Patsy J. Daniels

Dr. Patsy J. Daniels is Professor of English in the Department of English and Modern Foreign Languages at Jackson State University in Jackson, Mississippi. Dr. Daniels holds a Ph.D. in Literature and Criticism from Indiana University of Pennsylvania and is the Editor of *The Researcher: An Interdisciplinary Journal* based at Jackson State University.